INTERNATIONAL STUDIES
of the
Committee on International Relations
University of Notre Dame

INTERNATIONAL STUDIES

• Theoretical Aspects of International Relations, EDITED BY WILLIAM T. R. FOX • What America Stands For, EDITED BY STEPHEN D. KERTESZ AND M. A. FITZSIMONS • Diplomacy in a Changing World, EDITED BY STEPHEN D. KERTESZ AND M. A. FITZSIMONS • Introduction to Modern Politics, BY FERDINAND A. HERMENS • Freedom and Reform in Latin America, EDITED BY FREDERICK B. PIKE • The Russian Revolution and Religion, 1918-1925, EDITED BY BOLESLAW SZCZESNIAK • Soviet Policy Toward the Baltic States, BY ALBERT N. TARULIS • Catholicism, Nationalism, and Democracy in Argentina, BY JOHN J. KENNEDY • The Representative Republic, BY F. A. HERMENS • Why Democracies Fail: A Critical Evaluation of the Causes for Modern Dictatorship, BY NORMAN L. STAMPS • Christian Democracy in Western Europe, 1820-1953, BY MICHAEL P. FOGARTY • The Fate of East Central Europe: Hopes and Failures of American Foreign Policy, EDITED BY STEPHEN D. KERTESZ • German Protestants Face the Social Question, BY WILLIAM O. SHANAHAN • Diplomacy in a Whirlpool: Hungary Between Nazi Germany and Soviet Russia, BY STEPHEN D. KERTESZ • Soviet Imperialism: Its Origins and Tactics, EDITED BY WALDEMAR GURIAN • Pan-Slavism: Its History and Ideology, BY HANS KOHN • The Foreign Policy of the British Labour Government: 1945-1951, BY M. A. FITZSIMONS • Bolshevism: An Introduction to Soviet Communism, BY WALDEMAR GURIAN • Christian Democracy in Italy and France, BY MARIO EINAUDI AND FRANCOIS GOGUEL

Out of Print

• The Soviet Union: Background, Ideology, Reality, EDITED BY WALDEMAR GURIAN • The Catholic Church in World Affairs, EDITED BY WALDEMAR GURIAN AND M. A. FITZSIMONS • Europe Between Democracy and Anarchy, BY FERDINAND A. HERMENS

THEORETICAL ASPECTS OF INTERNATIONAL RELATIONS

Theoretical Aspects of International Relations

EDITED BY WILLIAM T. R. FOX

UNIVERSITY OF NOTRE DAME PRESS • 1959

© 1959
UNIVERSITY OF NOTRE DAME PRESS
NOTRE DAME, INDIANA

LIBRARY OF CONGRESS CATALOG CARD NUMBER 59-14677

Foreword

The Committee on International Relations has been concerned with the recurring dilemmas of liberal and democratic states in the formulation of foreign policy. In the course of this work we have come to recognize the importance of developing a theory to comprehend, explain, and guide the study of international relations and the formulation of foreign policy. Thus, the Committee is particularly pleased to have the opportunity of publishing the present symposium. The members of the Committee did not participate in it, but with this publication they hope to stimulate further inquiry to which the Committee intends to make a contribution.

Preface

One striking characteristic of the subject of international relations as a field of academic study is the lack of an agreed framework for theoretical inquiry. The title of this symposium volume of essays, *Theoretical Aspects of International Relations,* was chosen advisedly. It does not imply the existence of some central body of integrated international relations theory; yet it is perfectly compatible with a belief shared by all the contributors. International relations has to be viewed as a subject which is something more than contemporary history if it is to evolve as a legitimate academic specialty or is to yield results relevant to the major choices which governments and opinion leaders must make in world politics.

Dean Rusk and Kenneth W. Thompson of the Rockefeller Foundation invited a small group to meet in Washington in 1954 to discuss with them the prospects for developing theoretical investigations in the field of international relations. It included professors, practitioners, and publicists with a particular concern for international affairs.[1]

It shortly transpired that the participants were talking about several different kinds of theories. Each of the three, or possibly four, kinds of theory — "normative," "empirical and/or scientific" and "rational" — is exemplified in the essays which follow. Whatever labels were used, there seemed to be agreement as to the need both for clarification of norms and for ordering of events. Thus, the value

1. For an account of the conference and an analysis of its discussions, see Kenneth W. Thompson, "Toward a Theory of International Politics," *American Political Science Review,* XLIX (September 1955), 733-46. The participants, in addition to Messrs. Rusk and Thompson, were Robert Bowie, Dorothy Fosdick, William T. R. Fox, Walter Lippmann, Hans J. Morgenthau, Reinhold Niebuhr, Paul H. Nitze, Don K. Price, James B. Reston, and Arnold Wolfers.

of both normative and non-normative types of theorizing was generally recognized.

Only if those who professed a common interest in international relations theory could be brought to state their theoretical positions in terms so that the issues, if any, which divided them would be clearly defined, could lines of inquiry for clarifying problems and resolving differences be sketched out.

The contributors to the present symposium, most of whom attended the Washington meeting, were therefore asked to prepare papers on topics of their own choosing for discussion at an inter-university seminar which held three two-day meetings during 1957. The writers were limited in their choice of topics only by the requirement that their papers be suitable for discussion at a seminar dealing with theoretical aspects of international relations.

The Institute of War and Peace Studies of Columbia University was the host organization. As its Director, I was the chairman of the seminar. Dr. Kenneth N. Waltz, now of Swarthmore College, shared with me responsibility for planning the meetings and acted as general rapporteur. Six of the papers were presented as public lectures at Columbia University, most of them immediately prior to their discussion in the inter-university seminar.[2] In addition to the authors of the papers, fifteen other scholars, with theoretical interests in international relations and geographically located so that they could attend a series of meetings in New York, participated.[3] Each contributor has had the opportunity to revise his paper to whatever extent seminar discussion and further reflection have seemed to him to require.

The series of papers is not an orderly survey of the main problems of international relations theory. The decision to invite each participant to develop an essay on a topic of his own choosing precluded any effort to achieve systematic coverage.

Given the exploratory nature of the Washington meeting and the

2. The substance of the paper by Kenneth N. Waltz was presented to the seminar for discussion in March 1957; a revised version was read at a panel session of the American Political Science Association in September 1957.
3. Bernard Barber, Herbert A. Deane, Morton A. Kaplan, Laurence W. Martin, Arno J. Mayer, Yoshikazu Sakamoto, Burton M. Sapin, Warner R. Schilling, Glenn H. Snyder, Richard Sterling, John B. Stewart, Kenneth W. Thompson, Robert W. Tucker, Robert W. Tufts, and Martin Wight.

unresolved problems which were posed there, it would probably have been premature to make the effort to agree even on the form of a systematic survey; it would certainly have been impossible to agree on the content of such a survey.

The essays fall into three groups. The first group deals, not with substantive theoretical problems, but rather with the characteristics and uses of speculative analyses of international relations. The essays by Paul H. Nitze, Hans J. Morgenthau, and William T. R. Fox fall into this category.

The second group of essays examines the prospects for developing theories of international relations "from the outside." Kenneth N. Waltz surveys the classics of Western political thought as source material for clarifying international relations theory. Charles P. Kindleberger examines the possibility of developing in the field of international relations theoretical propositions comparable to those found in contemporary economic theory.

Finally, there are two essays which deal more or less directly with substantive theoretical problems. Arnold Wolfers discusses the theoretical implications of varying assumptions regarding the actor in international politics. Reinhold Niebuhr's essay is perhaps the only one in the symposium in which the preferences of the author in the field of public policy are at least implicitly suggested, and these preferences are grounded in his particular conceptual approach.

The present volume is only one of several which have in the decade of the 1950's reflected an increasing concern with intellectual activity which is described by those engaged in it as "theoretical." Not all the recent theoretical activity has taken the form of exegesis and evaluation of other people's theories of international relations. Thus, at least four former members of the policy planning staff in the Department of State have felt the need to set forth some of the theoretical and philosophical presuppositions on which they believe policy ought to be based.[4] Quincy Wright in *The Study of Interna-*

---

4. Dorothy Fosdick, *Common Sense and World Affairs* (New York, 1955); Louis J. Halle, *Choice for Survival* (New York, 1958) and *Civilization and Foreign Policy* (New York, 1955); George Frost Kennan, *American Diplomacy 1900-1950* (Chicago, 1951) and *Realities of American Foreign Policy* (Princeton, 1954); Charles Burton Marshall, *Limits of Foreign Policy* (New York, 1954).

tional Relations (1955) has striven to give shape and coherence to the whole field. John Herz has written two books which are explicitly theoretical, the second being an effort to state the implications for our state system of bipolarity and atomic-age weapons systems.[5] George Liska and Morton Kaplan are authors of *The International Equilibrium* (1957) and *System and Process in International Politics* (1957), respectively. Ernst Haas and Allen Whiting, in the preface to their recent text, *Dynamics of International Relations* (1956), indicate that they have followed theoretical orientations of Harold D. Lasswell, Karl Mannheim, Robert MacIver, and Max Weber.

The range of propositions variously described as theoretical is so broad that it would almost seem that any fairly general statement about world politics that is not palpably absurd would qualify. This is perhaps as it should be. We have been theorizing all the time. The need is for us to gain a greater theoretical self-awareness so that we can subject our theories to a more sustained and penetrating critical analysis.

A grant from the Rockefeller Foundation made it possible for the Institute of War and Peace Studies to organize the inter-university seminar before which these essays were all presented in draft form. The Committee on International Relations of the University of Notre Dame, under the chairmanship of Professor Stephen Kertesz, has made their publication possible. The editors of the *Review of Politics,* also published at Notre Dame, have been notably hospitable to authors of speculative analyses of world politics; it is therefore particularly appropriate for the essays to be published under Notre Dame auspices. I am grateful to both the Foundation and the Committee on International Relations, as I am also to my co-authors who without exception met the editor's deadline and must thereby have set a record almost without parallel in the publication of a symposium volume.

William T. R. Fox

Institute of War and Peace Studies
Columbia University, March 17, 1959

---

5. John H. Herz, *Political Realism and Political Idealism* (Chicago, 1951) and *International Politics in the Atomic Age* (New York, 1959).

TABLE OF CONTENTS

    Preface   ix

1. Necessary and Sufficient Elements of a General Theory of International Relations   1
   Paul H. Nitze
   Foreign Service Educational Foundation

2. The Nature and Limits of a Theory of International Relations   15
   Hans J. Morgenthau
   University of Chicago

3. The Uses of International Relations Theory   29
   William T. R. Fox
   Institute of War and Peace Studies
   Columbia University

4. Political Philosophy and the Study of International Relations   51
   Kenneth N. Waltz
   Swarthmore College

5. International Political Theory From Outside   69
   Charles P. Kindleberger
   Massachusetts Institute of Technology

6. The Actors in International Politics   83
   Arnold Wolfers
   The Washington Center of Foreign Policy Research

7. Power and Ideology in National and International Affairs   107
   Reinhold Niebuhr
   Union Theological Seminary

THEORETICAL ASPECTS OF
INTERNATIONAL RELATIONS

Chapter I

Necessary and Sufficient Elements of a General Theory of International Relations

BY PAUL H. NITZE

Discussions concerning a theory of international relations are apt to disclose what seems at first sight to be a paradox. On the one hand, they point to the need for a unifying conceptual framework comprising a manageably small number of conceptual elements and therefore for a high degree of abstraction. On the other hand, they point to the need to relate whatever system of concepts is used to the complex worlds of general politics, of history, of philosophy and religion, and eventually to the infinitely complex living world of reality. On further consideration, however, these two drives — for abstraction and simplification and for wide relation — may not really be in conflict. In fact they may be mutually supporting.

In the field of the natural sciences it is hard to imagine a more highly abstract, succinct, and "elegant" equation than Einstein's famous equation relating matter to energy — $E = MC^2$. But this equation is meaningless unless viewed as a part of the immensely complex world of modern physics and mathematics. And many believe that to really understand why C^2, the square of the velocity of light, should appear in an equation relating mass to energy, one must go back to very deep philosophical and even metaphysical grounds.

Let us accept for the moment the hypothesis that one of the tasks of a general theory of international relations is the discovery of a relatively small number of abstract concepts which bear some continuing relationships one to another, an understanding of which relationships helps to illuminate and make more understandable the complex body of data comprised in the concrete world of international relations. There is a certain presumption in favor of a more elegant approach to this task, than of a more complex approach. In other words, on general grounds a three-element approach is preferable to a three-hundred-element approach. Simplicity has a virtue in itself, and one should not want to include any more elements in a theoretical structure than are necessary. But in addition to the criterion of simplicity and elegance there is the criterion of sufficiency. We must ask ourselves whether we have included sufficient elements for our theory to bear a meaningful relationship to the body of data it is meant to illuminate. In other words, the problem is one not just of demonstrating that this element or that element is necessary to a theory of international relations. The problem is rather one of finding what elements, in conjunction, constitute a necessary and sufficient foundation for a meaningful theory.

After this brief introduction it may be appropriate to summarize briefly the major theses of the body of this paper. The first thesis will be that a general theory of international relations needs to deal with the relationships between at least three fundamental concepts. These are structure, purpose and situation. Power, and restraints on power, will be considered as subsidiary concepts within the system suggested by the three fundamental concepts. The second thesis will be that a general theory of international relations needs to permit of a multiplicity of viewpoints ranging from that of a responsible member of a particular group at a particular time (say, the Secretary of State of the United States today) to one that approximates, as far as may be possible, to that of a hypothetical observer from Mars studying the emergent characteristics of an interacting system of many cultures, races, states, classes, etc., over the full course of history. The third thesis will be that a general theory of international relations needs to deal with two realms, the realm of fact and the realm of value — of "should" propositions — and with the interrelations between these realms.

In conclusion, the paper will touch upon the relation of the insights of a general theory of international relations to general politics, to history, philosophy, and religion on the one hand and to the living world of concrete action on the other.

I

We are all familiar with the proposal that "power" be considered *the* central concept of political theory. We are also familiar with the counter-argument that equally important with power, and conceptually prior to it, is the concept of purpose — the purposes to which power is directed. My suggestion is that even before one talks about purpose one has to be clear about whose purpose it is one is referring to and on whose behalf that purpose is directed — and that this requires an analysis of political structure.

I take it that individuals participate simultaneously in a wide variety of group structures. I have worked with Mr. Dulles and know something of him as a man and of his life as the senior member of an able and vigorous family. I know something of his relations with the law firm of Sullivan and Cromwell. I know something of his position in the Republican Party, of his role as Secretary of State of the Government of the United States, something of his role as the senior statesman of NATO, OAS, SEATO, etc., and something of his relationship to the Church and to the National Council of Churches.

The loyalties, purposes, objectives, principles and policies of each of these groups are far from identical. In part they converge, or reinforce each other, in part they are in conflict and create tensions and issues of divided loyalty.

Every participant in today's international scene, be he Gromyko, Nasser, a member of the Damascus mob, or a voter in the Polish elections, has similar complex group affiliations.

In developing a theory of international relations particular emphasis may properly be put on the particular group entity, the nation-state, which is presumed to have achieved a monopoly of the legitimate use of coercive force within the established geographic limits of its jurisdiction. There is a strong presumption that where such an effective monopoly exists there have developed strong ethnic, cultural, or other ties stemming from a shared historical experience.

Incidentally I take it that the word "international" in our topic is merely suggestive and is not meant to exclude, for instance, relations between the Greek or the Italian city states in another historical period just because the prime political units were then city states not nations.

The point is rather that even in a period in which the nation-state is predominant it cannot be considered absolute. It makes a substantial difference in international politics what the other and sometimes competing group structures are, what is the strength of loyalties and sympathies which they evoke, what is the content of the value structures which are associated with them.

The affiliation of each individual to the particular national group of which he is a member is not necessarily so overwhelming as to overcome all other loyalties, even as they affect international relations. In those instances where the purposes and interests of a nation are clear and unambiguous, national affiliation tends to overwhelm other sympathies. But the purposes and interests of nations are not always clear and unambiguous. Furthermore, the effective formulation of what a nation's purposes and interests are conceived to be, is much influenced by loyalties and sympathies which spring from participation in social groupings both broader than, and narrower than, the prime political entity.

In extreme cases it is hard to know whether the concept "nation" has any validity at all. Hungary may be a nation, and the common and intense experience through which the Hungarian people passed, during and after their ill-fated revolution, may weld them even more closely together as a nation. But the Hungarian government is hardly a national government. When one speaks of the purpose or the power of Hungary, what is it one is referring to? Obviously the struggle for power between the Kadar regime, backed by Soviet military force, and the mass of the population was far more significant than the power relationships between Hungary (conceived as comprising both its government and its people) and other national groups.

At this point I might comment that while I take seriously Whitehead's admonition against misplaced assumptions of concreteness I do not share the horror that many social scientists appear to have about the danger of reification in the use of abstract concepts.

There is not any doubt in my mind that the United States is a nation, in a very real sense, and that India has in recent years become one. Even though the word "nation" may be difficult to define it would seem to me that there is in fact a very real thing to which it can refer.

My point, therefore, is not that the nation is unreal; my point is that there are other things which are also very real — your family, my family, Sullivan and Cromwell, the State Department, Western civilization, the Christian religion — and that every individual participates in a variety of such very real entities.

It seems to me essential that any general theory of international relations have in it room for the consideration of the interrelated structure of these entities, not usually coterminous with national boundaries, which make competing claims on the loyalties, purposes, and actions of individuals.

In almost every problem of international politics the first question to be asked is, in the particular context, who is to be regarded as the "we" and who is to be regarded as the "they."

When Mr. Khrushchev and Mr. Gromyko address themselves to the Middle East, who in their minds is the primary "we" group, what are the other "we" groups in whose behalf they consider themselves to be acting, and what are the structural relationships between those "we" groups? Is it not likely that they put first the "we" group of the Communist Party Bolshevik, that the Soviet Union as a nation they consider to be "we" but in a secondary, not a primary sense, that the communist parties in Syria, Egypt, etc., they consider to be "we" but in a tertiary sense, in the sense of instruments to be used rather than prime participants in the group on whose behalf policy is being executed?

Similarly on our side whom do Mr. Eisenhower and Mr. Dulles consider to be the prime "we" group? Who are the other "we" groups whose interests they must take into account? Where does the NATO alliance fit into this structure? Where does Israel fit into it? Where do the Arab States, India, or the generality of mankind fit into it?

A case can be made that the first question, of politics in general and of international politics in particular, is whether, in what contexts and to what degree, people consider themselves to be part of a common "we" or opposed as hostile "theys." In other words political structure would seem to be one of the necessary primary concepts of political theory.

II

Let us assume for the moment that the question of structure has been taken care of and that, in the given context, we are clear as to the "we" and "they" groups we are talking about and their interrelations. Now what can be said about the concept "purpose"?

Perhaps a more useful phrase is the phrase "Value System." If we examine the attitudes of any organized group, let us take as an example the United States, we find a rich and diversified panoply of means and of ends and of general principles dealing with the proper relationship of means to ends. As we examine the ends in greater detail we find that they sort themselves out in a hierarchical structure. Certain of the ends, when looked at from above, appear to be means to higher ends. Certain of the means, when looked at from below, appear to be ends in relation to still more subordinate means. As we examine the principles governing the relating of means to ends we find that these principles fit in intermediate positions, higher than certain of the ends and perhaps lower than other ends.

The United States today undoubtedly considers a first-class air force capability to be a desirable end. In relation to that end, base agreements with Spain and Saudi Arabia, for instance, are desirable means. A first-class air force capability is in turn a means to the higher objective of an adequate posture of general military strength. A posture of general military strength is one of the means, among others, to general power in the international scene. Further up in the means-end chain is a still higher end. It is that an international climate be preserved in which political groups, organized in the manner of and for purposes similar to those characterizing the United States, can survive and prosper.

In such an analysis the difficult problems arise at two points. The most difficult problem is reached as one approaches the top of such a hierarchy. What are the central values which comprise the ultimate, non-contingent values of the group? One of these is probably survival of the group as a group. But related to this is the problem of the essential character of the group, to change which would be in essence tantamount to non-survival of the group.

The second difficulty arises in fitting into the hierarchy the general principles relating means to ends.

Effective opinion in the United States believes that force should not be used to settle international disputes, that binding contractual obligations of the United States government should be honored, that governments should generally be responsive to the will of the governed. If we were to consider settlement of a dispute vital to our survival, and believed in a given instance that it could only be resolved by force, I am sure we would resolve it through the use of force. There are a number of binding contractual obligations which the government has violated and where, under the actual circumstances which existed, I believed it was quite justified in doing so. We tolerate and even assist governments which are hardly responsive to the will of their people, and for very good reason.

The point is that the principles relating means to ends fit within the means-end hierarchy at varying levels and are not to be taken as absolutes standing outside that hierarchy.

The word "purpose" is often used in differing senses. Sometimes it is used to refer to the central values of a group, the loss of which would be tantamount to non-survival of the group. In this sense it refers to the top part of the means-principles-ends hierarchy. Sometimes the word "purpose" is used to imply the entire means-principles-ends hierarchy. It is used in this second sense in this article. When "purpose" is used to refer to the entire means-principles-ends hierarchy applicable to any given political group, or system of interlocking political groups, it seems appropriate to view it as another of the fundamental concepts in a general theory of politics and thus of international relations.

III

From the standpoint of a value system applicable to a particular nation, say the United States, "power" takes on the aspect of an intermediate means-end. Many of the subsidiary ends of United States foreign policy can be considered as means to the higher end of an increase in the general power of the country. But this increase in power is in turn a means to support the more general ends of that policy. The main point about power is that it is fungible, that it can be directed to achieving any one of a number of ends including particular ends which are not foreseen in advance. It is this aspect of power, its fungibility, which justifies the analogy which is sometimes drawn between the role of power in a theory of international politics and wealth in economic theory.

Because of its fungible character, an increase in power tends to become the end upon which statesmen and others dealing with foreign policy focus when the more general aims of foreign policy become confused or doubtful. It is possible, therefore, to construct a theory of international relations which assumes that power is in fact the ultimate aim of national foreign policies and to find that the analysis which flows from such a theory gives certain valuable insights into the real world of international politics.

Clausewitz in discussing military strategy starts off with an analysis of the "pure" theory of war. This "pure" theory assumes that no outside policy considerations will mitigate the natural tendency of war to degenerate to the utmost violence which the then state of military technology makes possible. But having analyzed this "pure" theory and drawn from it certain insights, he follows up by saying that no actual war has ever been fought according to the "pure" theory, that none ever will be so fought, and that it would be pointless and meaningless to do so. He then devotes much of his book to firmly subordinating military policy to the more general aims of political policy and thus more directly relates his theory to reality.

Even though analogies are dangerous, I would suggest that political theory in its treatment of power has a problem analogous to that faced by Clausewitz.

From the standpoint of the analysis of value systems associated with political groups, "power" is to be viewed not as a fundamental analytical category but as a subordinate element of the concept "purpose." For certain types of analyses in the field of international politics it may be fruitful to reduce the entire means-ends hierarchy to a competitive search for power. To do this involves a simplification comparable to the assumption that the nation-state is the only meaningful structural entity in the international scene and that the other complex structural elements may be ignored. Such radical simplifications are only useful if the analyst is quite conscious of what it is he is doing. Otherwise such simplifications may become over-simplifications.

IV

Let us now turn to the third fundamental concept suggested in the introduction to this paper, namely, the concept "situation."

Any analysis of politics requires reference to the facts of the situation in which the political events are assumed to take place. The set of facts which are relevant in a given instance may vary widely. They may be facts of geography, demography, the state of scientific knowledge, the stage of economic development, the availability of natural resources, the power of given weapon systems, etc.

A problem arises as to how the cut-off line is to be determined between those facts and values which are to be included within the concepts of "structure" and "purpose" and those to be included within the concept "situation." The problem is analogous to that which one meets in mathematics in deciding which quantities are to be treated as variables and which quantities as parameters. It depends upon the field of interest of the observer. For the student of politics "structure" and "purpose" are at the center of his field of study and are generally to be treated as variables while climate, geography, or demography, for instance, are generally treated as parameters. These latter factors can change and in changing can modify the equations at issue but it is not these relationships which are usually the primary focus of interest of political theory. For the study of politics they can usually be assumed to have some reasonable but arbitrarily selected values so that the more interesting relations between the factors selected as variables can be explored.

V

At this point it may be helpful to say a few words about the second thesis mentioned in the introduction to this paper. This thesis is that a general theory of international relations needs to permit of a multiplicity of viewpoints, ranging from that of a responsible member of a particular group at a particular time to one that approximates, as far as may be possible, to that of a hypothetical observer from Mars studying the emergent characteristics of an interacting system of many cultures, races, states, classes, etc., over the full course of history.

If one attempts to get as close as possible to the viewpoint of the hypothetical man from Mars and looks at the classical period of the Greek city states, at the period of the Italian city states during the Renaissance, of the Warring States in early Chinese history or of the European national state system during its heyday, certain common characteristics appear to emerge. It makes sense to talk of a common cultural base within which each system operated. Certain characteristic restraints on the unlimited exercise of state power developed. There was a consciousness on the part of the leading statesmen that they were part of a common culture and a common political system, that penalties could be expected if they adopted courses of action too violently inimical to the maintenance of the system and finally that there were certain types of action which they ought not to take. From this exalted view the system as a whole takes on the aspect of a group with an associated value system and sense of purpose. Mr. Toynbee advocates a focus on the history of civilizations rather than nations on somewhat similar grounds.

If one starts from the other end of the spectrum and views the problems of international relations from the standpoint of a given individual at a given moment of history, one gets a somewhat different slant, but there is still a certain degree of convergence in the final result. Let us take as our individual a member of the Policy Planning Staff of the Department of State at today's moment of history. I take this example because it is one with which I have been personally familiar.

This individual by his oath of office is required to uphold the Constitution of the United States and the faithful execution of the laws. His primary obligation is, therefore, to the United States as a nation-state, its value system and purposes, and its institutions. In developing his recommendations to the Secretary of State, particularly on new issues — issues on which there is no body of tradition and no clear-cut guide lines have developed from previous national or Congressional debate on the subject — he finds himself being led into the most searching and difficult avenues of value analysis. To what extent should policy be made on the basis of a "we" group extending out to include the peoples and governments allied to us? To what extent should the interests of the entire free world be considered? Are there issues on which the interests of mankind as a whole should be considered? Are there judgments as to equity and justice which flow not merely from the desirability that the United States as an organized group survive? Where are the grounds for a solid judgment on questions of equity and justice to be found: in natural law? in philosophy? in religion? What are the margins of freedom available to the United States within which it is possible both to promote the interests of the United States as an organized political group and also to promote more general standards of justice?

The point is that the framework of a general theory of international relations should be broad enough to encompass both points of view and points of view lying in between these extremes.

VI

As we have seen from the previous section, value propositions enter into our analysis even when we start from the most diverse points of view, that of the individual contemporary actor and that of the hypothetical man from Mars surveying the full range of history.

Value propositions can enter into the analysis, moreover, in two different ways. They can enter into the analysis from the standpoint of the actor, in which case they are of the nature of "should" propositions constituting the internal criteria bearing upon his decisions. They can also enter into the analysis as part of the "situation" with which the actor has to deal. Soviet doctrine, to the man in the State Department, is an assembly of "should" propositions which he must treat as objective facts not materially subject to change by anything he can do. They enter into his decisions as part of the "situation" in which the action he is contemplating must take place, not as internal criteria. The value system associated with his own position by virtue of his being an American, a responsible member of the United States State Department, and the kind of person he is, enters into his decisions in an entirely different way. Its "should" propositions have with respect to him an ethical, an imperative, quality.

Even the man approaching problems from approximately the position of the man from Mars is faced with the task of making a distinction between those "should" propositions he treats as matters of fact and those he uses as criteria by which he expresses approval or disapproval of what the various actors did or might have done.

Thus the third thesis of this paper, that a general theory of international relations needs to deal with two realms, the realm of fact and the realm of value — of "should" propositions — may need further expansion to include the two separate ways in which "should" propositions can enter into the analysis.

VII

It remains to consider the question of restraints on power.

These restraints may be of two kinds. They may be in the "situation." The factors of geography, the state of technology, the distribution of military power, etc., may be such as to preclude the free exercise of power beyond certain limits. The restraints may, however, be of entirely different nature. They spring from the system of values impinging upon a broad aggregate of states and other actors. They may impinge upon action directly through influencing the internal value system of the actor being considered. They may also be part of the external situation which he must consider in making his decisions.

Reinhold Niebuhr in another essay in the present volume, "Power and Ideology in National and International Affairs," deals with the relative position of the values "order," "justice," and "freedom" in the value systems, not just of individual nations, but across whole periods of history. He continues with an analysis of how changes in the position of these values came about in Europe and suggests reasons why the rising commercial classes needed a flexible instrument of political authority and why they needed the prestige of justice as well as the prestige of being the instrument of order to maintain the particular form of political authority which they had evolved.

I am told that President Eisenhower when he was deciding what action the United States should take after the British and French intervened in Suez wrestled with two questions. The first question was whether aggression is now obsolete as a means of settling disputes. The second question was whether it is possible to reserve the use of force to those cases where its use has a common sanction within the affected group.

It is not the purpose of this paper to go into the substantive issues involved in trying to find reasonably precise answers to these two questions. The point that I wish to make here is that the leading responsible statesman of one of the great powers today feels that questions of this kind are basic to the day-to-day decisions he must make.

The United States is attempting to promote a tolerable degree of order in the vastly complex Middle Eastern situation. The instruments of physical force which it has available for application in that area are extremely limited or else inappropriate as instruments to be applied to political problems of the nature of those there to be dealt with and managed. The other instruments of United States power which can be applied are also limited. It naturally becomes of the utmost importance to achieve a high degree of consent to such actions as we take, particularly if we must ever use military force. The degree of consent which we need cannot be achieved unless there is a reasonably wide acceptance in the area that our actions conform to and unless they tend to achieve some form of justice. A situation has developed in which there are, therefore, very great restraints upon the use of United States force, and perhaps to a lesser degree, upon the free exercise of other elements of United States power.

The developments which are taking place today in the world of international affairs bear a certain resemblance to the internal political developments within the European states to which Dr. Niebuhr refers in his essay.

A general theory of international relations which does not provide an adequate framework for the analysis of restraints upon the free exercise of national power would, therefore, appear to be insufficient and not closely enough related to the real world of international politics and the questions with which statesmen do in fact wrestle.

VIII

There is nothing particularly novel about the approach to a general theory of international relations put forward in this paper. Much of what seems to me to be the best work in the field does in fact fit within the suggested framework. What perhaps is distinctive is a matter of emphasis; a conscious effort on the one hand to grapple with concepts of a high order of abstraction and their interrelation, and on the other hand to relate these abstract notions to the broader fields of general politics, of history, philosophy and religion. I believe that such a focus, if rigorously pursued, can open up new vistas of illumination. Without the use of abstract notions the field is far too complex to be grasped by the mind in any meaningful way. Without the relation to other fields the concepts become mushy and imprecise. The latter difficulty cannot be escaped merely by attempts at careful definition. The terms in which the definition is expressed generally lead back into broad areas of thought and of experience.

But let us suppose that we have made a certain degree of progress in our theoretical approach. How does one go about relating the insights obtained from theory to the world of practice? Here a process is involved which is the reverse of abstraction. Having cut off layer after layer of contingent detail in order to arrive at the essential core abstractions with which a theory can usefully deal, and having derived a certain insight from the manipulation of these abstract notions, we must then reverse the process and add layer after layer of contingent but relevant detail before we have something which may be applicable to the concrete world of human affairs. It is an accepted maxim that politics is an art and not a science. The final decision to take one course of action rather than another must be based on a human judgment involving a host of cross considerations. Judgments of this kind can only in part be based on rational intellectual processes. In large measure they must be a reflection of the character of the man, the nation, and the society that makes them. But there is still an element in the decision which is susceptible to human reasoning. And that reasoning can be better if it has available to it better theoretical and analytical tools than are available to it today. It is my belief that a general theory of international relations is possible and can supply such a tool.

Chapter II

THE NATURE AND LIMITS OF A THEORY OF INTERNATIONAL RELATIONS

BY HANS J. MORGENTHAU

I

THIS PAPER is based upon three assumptions: first, that for theoretical purposes international relations is identical with international politics; second, that a theory of international politics is but a specific instance of a general theory of politics; and that the latter is identical with political science.

1. International relations as the totality of social phenomena transcending national boundaries are no more susceptible to specific theoretical understanding than are "domestic" or "national" relations. Both comprising the totality of social relations of a general type, they can only be understood in terms of a general theory of society. Only a general sociological system could do justice to such a conception of international relations. Any less ambitious theoretical endeavor cannot help but focus upon a particular element of international relations. That focus must be determined by the intellectual interest of the observer. What is it we want to know about international relations? What concerns us most about it? What questions do we want a theory of international relations to answer? The answers to these questions determine the content of a specific theory of international relations, and the answers may well differ not only from one period of history to another, but from one contemporaneous group of observers to another.

Hypothetically one can imagine as many theories of international relations as there are legitimate intellectual perspectives from which to approach the international scene. But in a particular culture and a particular period of history, one perspective is likely, for theoretical and practical reasons, to take precedence over the others. This perspective today is international politics.

2. A theory of international politics is but a specific instance of a general theory of politics. What is true of the latter is, *mutatis mutandis,* also true of the former. The issues with which a general political theory must come to terms confront also a theory of international politics. The differences between both do not result from their theoretical structure, which is common to both, but only from the peculiarities of their respective subject matters.

International politics being but a specific instance of a general political theory, the main task is to understand the requirements and problems of such a theory. For if this assumption is correct, the key to a theory of international politics will not be found in the specific subject matter of international politics but in the requirements and problems of a general political theory.

We must, then, ask: I. What are the requirements of political theory? II. What are the problems which call into question the possibility of political theory? III. How does the subject matter of international politics modify the general requirements and problems of political theory?

3. Perhaps no event has had a more disastrous effect upon the development of political science than the dichotomy between political theory and political science. For it has made political theory sterile by cutting it off from contact with the contemporary issues of politics, and it has tended to deprive political science of intellectual content by severing its ties with the Western tradition of political thought, its concerns, its accumulation of wisdom and knowledge.

The very distinction between political theory and political science is untenable. Science is theoretical, or it is nothing. Historically and logically, a scientific theory is a system of empirically verifiable, general truths, sought for their own sake. This definition sets theory apart from practical knowledge, common-sense knowledge, and philosophy. Practical knowledge is interested only in truths which lend themselves to immediate practical application; common-sense knowledge is particular, fragmentary, and unsystematic; philosophic knowledge may be, but is not of necessity, empirically verifiable. What else, then, is scientific knowledge if not theory?

II

By making power its central concept, a theory of politics does not presume that none but power relations control political action. What it must presume is the need for a central concept which allows the observer to distinguish the field of politics from other social spheres, to orient himself in the maze of empirical phenomena which make up the field of politics, and to establish a measure of rational order within it. A central concept, such as power, then provides a kind of rational outline of politics, a map of the political scene. Such a map does not provide a complete description of the political landscape as it is in a particular period of history. It rather provides the timeless features of its geography distinct from their ever-changing historic setting. Such a map, then, will tell us what are the rational possibilities for travel from one spot on the map to another, and which road is most likely to be taken by certain travelers under certain conditions. Thus it imparts a measure of rational order to the observing mind and, by doing so, establishes one of the conditions for successful action.

A theory of politics, by the very fact of painting a rational picture of the political scene, points to the contrast between what the political scene actually is and what it tends to be, but can never completely become. The difference between the empirical reality of politics and a theory of politics is like the difference between a photograph and a painted portrait. The photograph shows everything that can be seen by the naked eye. The painted portrait does not show everything that can be seen by the naked eye, but it shows one thing that the naked eye cannot see: the human essence of the person portrayed. Thus a theory of politics must seek to depict the rational essence of its subject matter.

By doing so, a theory of politics cannot help implying that the rational elements of politics are superior in value to the contingent ones and that they are so in two respects. They are so in view of the theoretical understanding which the theory seeks; for its very possibility and the extent to which it is possible depend upon the rationality of its subject matter. A theory of politics must value that rational nature of its subject matter also for practical reasons. It must assume that rational policy is of necessity good policy; for only such a policy minimizes risks and maximizes benefits and, hence, complies both with the moral precept of prudence and the political requirement of success. A theory of politics must want the photographic picture of the political scene to resemble as much as possible its painted portrait.

Hence, a theory of politics presents not only a guide to understanding, but also an ideal for action. It presents a map of the political scene not only in order to understand what that scene is like, but also in order to show the shortest and safest road to a given objective. The use of theory, then, is not limited to rational explanation and anticipation. A theory of politics also contains a normative element.

These observations assume that an empirical theory of politics is possible. Yet the correctness of this assumption must be established against the formidable and popular opposition which is grounded in a relativist conception of man and society.

The same philosophic position which has made political science separate itself from theory has also made it deny the existence and intelligibility of objective, general truths in matters political. That denial manifests itself in different ways on different levels of discourse. On the level of the general theory of democracy, it leads to the conclusion that the decision of the majority is the ultimate datum beyond which neither analysis nor evaluation can go. On the level of the analyses of political processes and decisions, it reduces political science to the explanation of the ways by which pressure groups operate and the decisions of government are reached. A political science thus conceived limits itself to the descriptive analysis of a complex of particular historic facts. Its denial of the existence and intelligibility of a truth about matters political that exists regardless of time and place implies a denial of the possibility of political theory both in its analytical and normative sense. What a political science of the past has discovered to be true, then, is true only in view of the peculiar and ephemeral historic circumstances of the times, carrying no lesson for us or any other period of history, or else is a mere reflection of the subjective preferences of the observer. The political science of the past is thus reduced, insofar as it seeks empirical analysis, to the description of an ephemeral historic situation and, as normative theory, becomes undistinguishable from political ideology. This being so, contemporary political science is caught in the same relativism and is no more able to transcend the limitations of time and place than were its predecessors.

We cannot here enter into a detailed discussion of this fundamental problem; two observations must suffice. Political science, like any science, presupposes the existence and accessibility of objective, general truth. If nothing that is true regardless of time and place could be said about matters political, political science itself would be impossible. Yet the whole history of political thought is a living monument to that possibility. The relevance for ourselves of insights which political scientists of the past, reflecting upon matters political under the most diverse historic circumstances, considered to be true points toward the existence of a store of objective, general truths which are as accessible to us as they were to our predecessors. If it were otherwise, how could we not only understand, but also appreciate, the political insights of a Jeremiah, a Kautilya, a Plato, a Bodin, or a Hobbes?

Yet while common sense militates against the relativist conception of political science, two perennial problems lend apparent support to such a conception by calling into question the possibility of an empirical theory of politics and limiting its realization. One of these problems lies in the subject matter of politics; the other, in the peculiar position of the observer of the political scene.

III

What has stood in the way of the development of such an empirical theory of politics is the same formidable difficulty which has frustrated the attempts to develop a theory of history: the ambiguity of the material with which the theoretician must deal. This material consists of events which are, on the one hand, unique occurrences that happened in this way only once and never before or since. As such, they are beyond the grasp of theory. On the other hand, these same events are also specific instances of general propositions, and it is only as such that they are susceptible to theoretical understanding. It is the task of theory to detect in the welter of the unique facts of experience that which is uniform, similar, and typical. It is its task to reduce the facts of experience to mere specific instances of general propositions, to detect behind them the general laws to which they owe their existence and which determine their development.

Yet where is the line to be drawn between the unique and the general in that sphere of experience which we call politics? Two events in this sphere may be alike in certain respects; they will never be alike in all respects. How do the differences between the two situations influence the validity of the theoretical proposition which we might have developed from one of them? We might have learned from one situation that it is wrong to make concessions to an imperialistic nation or to intervene in a war between two other nations. Obviously, it cannot follow that one ought never to make concessions to an imperialistic nation nor intervene in a war between two other nations. A theoretical proposition is correct only under the assumption that all the relevant elements in the situation which have given rise to it are present in another situation and that no new circumstances have intervened, modifying their relevance. But how do we know with any degree of certainty which elements in the first situation are relevant to the theoretical proposition, whether these elements are present in the second situation, and what new elements in the second situation counteract the others? Here we can only play by ear and must be satisfied with a series of hunches which may or may not turn out to be correct.

A theory of politics must, then, guard against the temptation to take itself too seriously and to neglect the ambiguities which call it into question at every turn. A theory of politics which yields to that temptation becomes a metaphysics, superimposing a logically coherent intellectual scheme upon a reality which falls far short of such coherence and concealing its lack of cognitive relevance behind a veil of abstract propositions which have paid for their apparent precision with the elimination of concrete content. A theory of politics, to be theoretically valid, must build into its theoretical structure, as it were, those very qualifications which limit its theoretical validity and practical usefulness.

What makes a theory of politics possible in spite of the ambiguities of its subject matter is the rationality in which both the mind of the observer and the object of observation, that is, politics, partake. Politics is engaged in by rational men who pursue certain rational interests with rational means. The observer, however handicapped by the ambiguities referred to above, is able, by virtue of his own rationality, to retrace the steps which politics has taken in the past and to anticipate those it will take in the future. Knowing that behind these steps there is a rational mind like his own, the observer can put himself into the place of the statesman — past, present, or future — and think as he has thought or is likely to think. This rationality, which the observer of the political scene and that scene have in common, makes both the history and practice of politics possible. It also makes a theory of politics possible. A theory of politics is a rationally ordered summary of all the rational elements which the observer has found in the subject matter.

IV

The political world poses still another obstacle to theoretical understanding. This obstacle is of a moral rather than intellectual nature.

The moral position of the political scientist in society is ambivalent; it can even be called paradoxical. For the political scientist is a product of the society which it is his mission to understand. He is also an active part, and frequently seeks to be a leading part, of that society. To be faithful to his mission he would, then, have to overcome two limitations: the limitation of origin, which determines the perspective from which he looks at society, and the limitation of purpose, which makes him wish to remain a member in good standing of that society or even to play a leading role in it.

The mind of the political scientist is molded by the society which he observes. His outlook, his intellectual interests, and his mode of thinking are determined by the civilization, the national community, and all the particular religious, political, economic and social groups of which he is a member. The "personal equation" of the political scientist both limits and directs his scholarly pursuits. The truth which a mind thus socially conditioned is able to grasp is likewise socially conditioned. The perspective of the observer determines what can be known and how it is to be understood. In consequence, the truth of political science is of necessity a partial truth.

Upon a mind which by its very nature is unable to see more than part of the truth, society exerts its pressures, which confront the scholar with a choice between social advantage and the truth.

The stronger the trend toward conformity within the society and the stronger the social ambitions within the individual scholar, the greater will be the temptation to sacrifice the moral commitment to the truth for social advantage. It follows that a respectable political science — respectable, that is, in terms of the society to be investigated — is in a sense a contradiction in terms. For a political science which is faithful to its moral commitment of telling the truth about the political world cannot help telling society things it does not want to hear. The truth of political science is the truth about power, its manifestations, its configurations, its limitations, its implications, its laws. Yet one of the main purposes of society is to conceal these truths from its members. That concealment, that elaborate and subtle and purposeful misunderstanding of the nature of political man and of political society, is one of the cornerstones upon which all societies are founded.

A political science which is true to its moral commitment ought at the very least to be an unpopular undertaking. At its very best, it cannot help being a subversive and revolutionary force with regard to certain vested interests — intellectual, political, economic, social in general. For it must sit in continuous judgment upon political man and political society, measuring their truth, which is in good part a social convention, by its own. In doing so, it becomes an embarrassment to society intellectually. But it also becomes a political threat to the defenders or the opponents of the status quo or to both; for the social conventions about power, which political science cannot help subjecting to a critical — and often destructive — examination, are one of the main sources from which the claims to power, and hence power itself, derive.

It stands to reason that political science as a social institution could never hope even to approach this ideal of a completely disinterested commitment to the truth. For no social institution can completely transcend the limitations of its origin, nor can it endeavor to free itself completely from its commitment to the society of which it forms a part, without destroying itself in the attempt. Only rare individuals have achieved the Socratic distinction of unpopularity, social ostracism, and criminal penalties, which are the reward of constant dedication to the relevant truth in matters political. Yet while political science as a social institution cannot hope even to approach the ideal, it must be aware of its existence; and the awareness of its moral commitment to the truth must mitigate the limitations of origin as well as the compromises between the moral commitment and social convenience and ambition, both of which no political scientist can fully escape.

V

One basic fact distinguishes international politics from the domestic and other types of politics and exerts a persuasive influence on the practice of international politics as well as upon its theoretical understanding. That fact concerns the relationship between international society and its constituent members, the nation states. The constituent members of domestic society, individuals and subnational groups, live in an integrated society, which holds supreme power and is the repository of the highest secular values and the recipient of the ultimate secular loyalties. Yet these domestic societies are the constituent members of international society which must defer to them in terms of power, values, and loyalties. What sets international society apart from other societies is the fact that its strength — political, moral, social — is concentrated in its members, its own weakness being the reflection of that strength.

A theory of international politics has the task, in applying the general principles of politics to the international sphere, to reformulate, modify, and qualify these principles in the light of that distinctive quality of international politics. A theory of international politics plays, as it were, the tune which the general theory of politics provides, but it plays it in a key and with variations which stem from the peculiarities of international society. The national interest defined in terms of power, the precarious uncertainty of the international balance of power, the weakness of international morality, the decentralized character of international law, the deceptiveness of ideologies, the inner contradictions of international organization, the democratic control of foreign policy, the requirements of diplomacy, the problem of war — of these phenomena and problems of international politics theory must take account in terms of the general principles of politics, which reveal themselves on the international scene in peculiar manifestations, owing to the peculiar character of international society.

This is obviously not the place to attempt a demonstration of the correctness of this view; for such a demonstration would require the development of a substantive theory of international politics. Since the attempt to do this has been made elsewhere and since we are dealing here with the requirements and problems of such a theory rather than with its substance, it must suffice to point to the great and peculiar difficulties which stand in the way of the development of such a theory and to the relatively narrow limits within which it seems to be possible. Two facts deserve special attention in this context: the implicit rather than explicit character of past attempts at a theory of international politics, and the peculiar difficulties impeding theoretical understanding, which arise from the relationship of power, morality, and the national interest as it reveals itself on the international scene.

VI

That men throughout the ages have thought little of a theory of international politics is borne out by the fact that but rarely has an explicit attempt to develop such a theory been made; as rare instances of such attempts, Kautilya and Machiavelli come to mind. Men have generally dealt with international politics on one of three levels, all alien to theory: history, reform, or pragmatic manipulation. That is to say, they have endeavored to detect the facts and meaning of international politics through the knowledge of the past; or they have tried to devise a pattern of international politics more in keeping with an abstract ideal than the empirical one; or they have sought to meet the day-by-day issues of international politics by trial and error.

Yet each of these approaches presupposes, and in actuality reveals, a theoretical conception of what international politics is all about, however fragmentary, implicit, and unavowed such a theoretical conception may be. In historians with a philosophic bent, such as Thucydides and Ranke, the history of foreign policy appears as a mere demonstration of certain theoretical assumptions which are always present beneath the surface of historic events to provide the standards for their selection and to give them meaning. In such historians of international politics, theory is like the skeleton which, invisible to the naked eye, gives form and function to the body. What distinguishes such a history of international politics from a theory is not so much its substance as its form. The historian presents his theory in the form of a historical recital using the historic sequence of events as demonstration of his theory. The theoretician, dispensing with the historical recital, makes the theory explicit and uses historic facts in bits and pieces to demonstrate his theory.

What holds true of the historian of international politics applies also to the reformer. He is, as it were, a "forward-looking" theoretician. His scheme of reform provides an explicit theory of what international politics ought to be, derived from an explicit or implicit theory of what international politics actually is. What has prevented William Penn, the Abbé de St. Pierre, or contemporary World Federalists from developing a complete theory of international politics is their primary concern with practical reform rather than the absence of theoretical elements in their thinking.

It is this same practical concern which has prevented the practitioners of international politics from developing an explicit theory of what they are doing. Even a perfunctory perusal of the speeches, state papers, and memoirs of such diverse types of statesmen as Bismarck, Wilson, Churchill, and Stalin, shows that their relationship to theory is even closer than we found that of the historian to be. For the great statesman differs from the run-of-the-mill diplomatist and politician exactly in that he is able to see the issues confronting him as special cases of general and objective — that is, theoretical — propositions. Here again it is not the substance of his thinking, but the form in which it manifests itself, which distinguishes the statesman from the theoretician of international politics. Here again it is his practical concern, not his alienation from theory as such, which prevents him from becoming a theoretician. Yet it illuminates the theoretical essence of the statesman's thinking that whenever practical concerns receded into the background or seemed best served by theoretical considerations, the four great statesmen mentioned above naturally transformed themselves from practitioners into theoreticians, making explicit in systematic or aphoristic form the theoretical foundations of their statecraft.

These observations support the case for the possibility and even the necessity of the theoretical understanding of international politics. However, by showing the scarcity of explicit, systematic theories of international politics, they point to the difficulties which stand in the way of the development of such a theory. The relationship of power, morality, and the national interest constitutes one of these difficulties.

VII

On the domestic plane, the relationship among power, morality, and interest is so obvious as to be hardly open to controversy. In domestic politics, individuals pursue their interests defined in terms of power. These interests, in view of their relation to power, have three outstanding characteristics. First, the interests to which power attaches itself and which it serves are as varied and manifold as are the possible social objectives of the members of a given society. Second, these interests shift continuously from the center of political attention and emphasis to their margin until they may fade out of the political picture altogether, only to come back again when circumstances change. Third, measured by the interests of society as a whole, these interests are partial in nature, and their existence within a transcendent whole both determines their nature and limits the manner of their pursuit. The very nature of the interests with which the member of a domestic society may identify himself is determined by the "common good" as society as a whole understands it, and so are the means by which he may pursue those interests.

The relationship between interest and power is different on the international plane. Here power is wedded to the interests of a particular nation. And while it is true, as has been pointed out elsewhere, that it has not always been so and it is not likely to be so forever, the relatively constant and at present insoluble relationship between power and the national interest is the basic datum for purposes of both theoretical analysis and political practice. The content of the national interest is likewise constant over long periods of history. All the ideal and material elements which make up that content are subordinated at the very least to those requirements—not susceptible to rapid change —upon which the survival of the nation and the preservation of its identity depend. Finally—and most importantly—the national interest is not a fraction of a transcendent, comprehensive social interest to which it is subordinated and by which it is limited both as to content and as to the means employed for its realization. The period of history when the national interest could be said to be so subordinated and limited has been replaced by one in which the nation has become the highest secular social organization and its interest the common focus of secular social interests.

However, it is not these characteristics of the national interest which make theoretical understanding difficult. Quite to the contrary, the constancy and supremacy of the national interest, taken by themselves, favor theoretical analysis. Theoretical complications arise from the relationship which exists between morality, on the one hand, and power and the national interest, on the other. Here again it is instructive to trace the different manifestations of the same theoretical structure in the domestic and international sphere.

The relationship between morality, on the one hand, and power and interest, on the other, is threefold. First, morality limits the interests that power seeks and the means that power employs to that end. Certain ends cannot be pursued and certain means cannot be employed in a given society within a certain period of history by virtue of the moral opprobrium that attaches to them. Second, morality puts the stamp of its approval upon certain ends and means which thereby not only become politically feasible, but also acquire a positive moral value. These moral values, then, become an intrinsic element of the very interests that power seeks. Third, morality serves interests and power as their ideological justification.

In the domestic sphere morality performs all these three functions effectively. It directs the choice of the means and ends of power away from what society considers to be harmful to its purposes and towards what it regards to be beneficial to them. What we call a civilized political community is the result of the efficiency with which morality performs these negative and positive functions. Yet civilization requires more than the negative and positive limitations of the means and ends of politics. It also requires the mitigation of the struggle for power by glossing over power interests and power relations and making them appear as something different than what they actually are.

This ideological function, which morality performs on the domestic scene together with the other two, has become its main function for international politics. On the international scene, the individual nation is by far the strongest moral force, and the limitations which a supranational morality is able to impose today upon international politics are both fewer and weaker than they were almost at any time since the end of the Thirty Years' War. The individual nation, thus having become virtually the highest moral unit on earth, has naturally been tempted to equate its own moral values with morality as such, and especially the most powerful nations have found it hard to resist that temptation. In consequence, the main function which morality performs today for international politics is ideological. It makes it appear as though the interests and policies of individual nations were the manifestations of universal moral principles. The part aspires to become the whole, and there is very little to counteract that aspiration. It is not so much morality which limits individual interests, as it is the individual interests which identify themselves with morality.

This identification of the interests and power of the nation with universal morality confronts theoretical understanding with formidable difficulties. The distinction between ideology and morality becomes blurred, and so becomes the distinction between ideology and theory. The advocate of the national crusade appears not only to promote universal moral values, but also to have discovered theoretical truth. By contrast, the theoretician who seeks the truth hidden beneath these veils of ideology cannot help being in an intellectually and morally awkward position. His very probing of the moral pretenses of national interest and national power in the name of a higher truth and a higher morality makes him suspect of being indifferent to all truth and all morality.

Thus to develop a theory of international politics is not an easy thing. Perhaps this is why we have so many ideologies, and so few theories, of international politics.

Chapter III

THE USES OF INTERNATIONAL RELATIONS THEORY

BY WILLIAM T. R. FOX

I

WHY SHOULD anyone expect an international relations theorist to be useful? Isn't his function to be omniscient and disinterested? The answer to the second question provides the answer to the first. By not allowing his interests to cloud his vision, the student of international relations can make the observations of world politics which permit him to advance disinterested theories to account for and explain these observations. Thus, these disinterested conclusions help the policy-maker act with greater rationality to implement his values.

The scholar's interest ought not to influence his observations or his conclusions, but it certainly influences his selection of problems. Thus, the greater the value consensus between the theorist and the policy-maker, the greater the use of theory to policy. Given this value consensus, it is difficult for a social scientist to discover a problem worthy of his concentrated effort at solution which is not policy-relevant. Debate about the use of international relations studies often turns on whether or not research and theorizing ought to be "policy-oriented." This is largely a false issue.

Let us examine some speculative or theoretical analyses in order to demonstrate their actual or potential policy relevance. E. H. Carr's *The Twenty Years' Crisis*[1] counsels against those who try hard to buck the tides of history. For Carr, policy is seen as skillful adjustment, with the fewest broken heads possible, to the basic changes that are going

1. London, 1939.

to take place in world politics anyway. It is good advice, and is thus broadly policy-relevant, for those with too much zeal and too little humility as to the possibility of man becoming master of his own destiny. No more than any other general analysis ought it to have been used as a device for reading over-all policy directly from one's general theory of world politics. When it was first published in the months after the Munich crisis, it was possible to read this pioneering analysis as a polemical document in the appeasement debate. This, however, is a misuse of international relations theory, for it would have taken extensive and detailed analysis of the European political scene at the time of the Munich crisis, and possibly even the advantage of hindsight, to show whether the policy of the Chamberlain government was skillful adjustment or surrender of the most fundamental national interest.

More specifically policy-oriented was Nicholas J. Spykman's *America's Strategy in World Politics*.[2] Professor Spykman was in fact shooting at a moving target. His manuscript took shape during a period in which the Nazi menace over Europe after June 1940 had shaken the confidence of even the staunchest isolationist in America's capacity to stand alone. The isolationist then often adopted one of two variants of his isolationist position, quarter-sphere defense or hemisphere defense. It was this particular midsummer madness to which Spykman addressed himself. He assumed the existence of a two-state world, the Old World and the New World, and then demonstrated to his own satisfaction that the Old could conquer the New. If, he concluded, you do not want that to happen, you must, to the extent necessary, intervene in the Old World to prevent its being dominated by some one power or combination of powers. By the time the book was published, the attack at Pearl Harbor had cut off public debate in the United States about the merits of intervention. The Spykman book was not, however, without effect. Not only did this and similar works help to define the meaning of the war effort into which the United States had with every show of reluctance been dragged, but they helped to deflate in advance some of the exaggerated expectations as to what victory would bring. Thus, the Spykman type of analysis, like that of Carr, helped to clarify choice by limiting it.

2. New York, 1942.

The result of social science theorizing is not always to constrict the range of choice which official and other influential elites see as open to them. In delimiting the possible for those who must select a course of action, the theorist may also shed light on recently proposed policy alternatives and sometimes even direct attention to courses of action previously unimagined or imagined to be impossible.

The effect of social science theorizing is not always to constrict the range of choice which official and other influential elites see as open to them. Thus, in his task of delimiting the possible the theorist may point to an expanded range of choice made possible by a more systematic exploitation of newly available means for achieving objectives. Modern mass media, for example, enable foreign relations to be conducted by communications addressed to opinion groups in foreign countries other than the government itself. Woodrow Wilson's appeal to the dissident nationalities of the old Austro-Hungarian Empire hastened the demise of that empire. In his time he was using an abnormal weapon, and using it to win a war. To make psychological strategy a "normal" adjunct of policy and thus to utilize modern mass media efficiently, whether in war or in peace, in the service of a nation's foreign policy, one has to have a theoretical model of world politics less simple than that of billiard balls of varying sizes, called "great powers" and "small powers," bouncing against each other on a green baize table called "power politics."

Without closely reasoned theories of international relations, social scientists can indeed render a disservice to foreign policy-makers and other persons of influence by beckoning them up false paths, i.e., by seeming to make their range of choice greater or smaller than it really is. Slogans and clichés, and also the findings of modern social science which would work miracles if only the world would hold still long enough for the reform based on those findings to take effect, are no substitute for such theories. "Tensions breed war," but it by no means follows that every unilateral reduction in tension contributes to peace or to whatever values a government is trying to promote. Anything which relaxed tensions against Hitler in France, Britain and America during the 1930's, for example, contributed to making a big war inevitable, although it undoubtedly reduced the prospect of war at the moment.

For an analysis of the relation between tensions and war to be prescriptively useful, distinctions have to be developed. There is a difference between a selective relaxation of tension with respect to values that are not really threatened or are not really very valuable and a general relaxation which, if unilateral, might even be an invitation to aggression. There is a difference between demonstrating that an all-round reduction in tensions once achieved, would promote peace and security and showing, even if only in theory, how a staged reduction on a multilateral basis could provide a secure and peaceful transition to the new world of low-tension moral disarmament.

It would be easy to caricature and parody the prescriptions for saving the world which have from time to time been advanced by otherwise serious students of the social sciences whose views of world politics are uninformed by any tenable underlying theory. It would be easy; it would be amusing; but it might not be rewarding. The theorist then has his uses as a policeman to prevent other social scientists from crashing directly into the councils of high policy. He has a more positive function of orchestrating their insights into a symphony of understanding.[3]

The international relations theorist is, however, inadequately equipped for the task of providing a complete prescription for policy. He is likely to lack up-to-the-minute information, "contacts" to bring his information up to the minute, access to the final decision-maker, and skill in effective writing addressed to persons of lesser influence. If a first-class international relations scholar tries too hard to be *immediately* useful, he may only succeed in becoming a fourth-class journalist. He has a role as long as he acts as a social scientist. This social science role he abandons if he becomes a peddler of "current events" or an apologist for the reigning priests of high policy.

Theories are policy-relevant even in those cases in which the theories verge on the absurd. Thus, the spacists and the racists — with their theories whose empirical referents were shrouded in mystery and whose normative ambiguities made it impossible to disentangle their predictions and their preferences — were policy-relevant even though the purveyors of false theories. They are policy-relevant, whether they want to be or not, because their teaching and their preaching become

3. Cf. Kenneth N. Waltz, *Man, the State and War* (in press) (New York, 1959), ch. 3.

part of the world political process on whose future they are supposed to be shedding light. The "decline of the West," for example, based on some belief that civilizations, like forms of higher life, pass through a natural life-cycle of birth, growth, maturity, decay and death, could be a self-confirming hypothesis to the extent that it promoted fatalism among those who under other circumstances might have thought the West had a future.

Similarly, some professional students of international relations in the United States in the 1920's tended to define the American choice in foreign policy as being between selfish isolationism and unselfish internationalism, between withdrawal from Europe and membership in the League of Nations. Those who might have chosen to support a policy based on the enlightened self-interest of continued American participation in maintaining the European order were not always provided with the theoretical basis for developing their position. Thus, in a negative way as well as in a positive way, international relations scholarship was policy-relevant even in the heyday of isolationism. It can lead or it can mislead, but it cannot help making a difference.

It is a short step to argue that if the theorist's work makes a difference willy-nilly, it behooves the international relations scholar to make sure that he is not accidentally affecting the future in ways he does not desire and that, within the limits of opportunity, he is affecting it in ways he regards as benign. To do this he may have to be somewhat more explicit in stating to himself and to his readers the basis for his selection of topics to investigate and the relevance of his conclusions to problems of public policy. Whether or not there is need for more theory, there is a need for theory to be more explicitly formulated.

II

The recent burst of activity which is unambiguously labelled "theoretical," might seem to imply that whatever intellectual activity was going on before, it was not sufficiently theoretical. What is this theory of international relations to which such frequent reference is being made? There is no body of propositions conventionally called "international relations theory" in the sense that there is "economic theory," nor is the history of international relations thought frequently taught under the course title, "international relations theory," the way the history of political thought is taught under the course title, "political theory." However, like the child who only discovers when he goes to school that he has been speaking English all the time, we students of international relations may discover that we have been theorizing all the time. None of us would have been willing in the pre-theory period to have our research described as "rootless empiricism," and what but some theory or other would have enabled us to avoid being written off as mere accumulators of facts? And how can what looks superficially like a jumble of data be ordered except by some theories of classification and interrelatedness? And how can we make statements about what our data "means" unless we have some theories as to what may be legitimately inferred from the data, and how these inferences may be related to other inferences based on other observations of the real world by other investigators?

On the other hand, let none of us fall into the opposite trap of ever imagining that what we are engaged in is pure theorizing. Try as we may to avoid it, and I for one hope we do not try very hard, there are always real or imagined empirical referents which a given theory allegedly illuminates.[4] It takes both carbon and oxygen, both digestion and respiration to maintain life. Similarly, it takes both "facts" and "theories" to achieve understanding of the world in which nations and states are born and die, compete and cooperate, live at war or at peace.

Theory is not an end in itself any more than data-collecting is an end in itself. The world in which we dwell does not exist simply to provide empirical verification for the plausibility of our theories. At the same time it cannot be understood by random, seriatim observations uninformed by any disciplined ordering of the observations.

III

The recent rise in interest in both theory and doctrine[5] may be

4. The distinction between "theory" and "research" which is here implied is not as black and white as the discussion suggests. An extremely general statement is incapable of direct empirical verification. An extremely specific statement is meaningless unless it is capable of such verification; but there is no clear line between "generality" and "specificity" of statement.
5. It is desirable to distinguish between statements about what is, has been, might have been, will be, may be, or would be under specified conditions, and statements about what ought to be. Both types of propositions are included

accounted for in a variety of ways: its narrow usefulness to the prestige-hungry scholar, its contribution to political science, and its hoped for contribution to wiser choices in public policy.

(1) The student of international relations is sensitive to the charge that he has no "theory" and has no history either. If he asserts that his analyses are policy-oriented, he may be told that pimping and pandering for the artificers of high policy in Washington or London or Moscow is not "scholarship" and in fact undermines objectivity. Stated bluntly, the international relations scholar would feel less inferior if he had a body of propositions as difficult for his colleagues to understand and evaluate as some of theirs are for him. Paradoxically, this stimulus to theorizing might make international relations studies less useful to the policy-maker; it would certainly make them less immediately useful.

(2) With the increasing emphasis in political science on the *process* of politics rather than simply on the *form* of institutions, the study of world politics as "politics in the absence of government," can be more easily understood as organically related to the classical study of political science. The fashion of referring to some or all of the social sciences as "behavioral sciences" or "policy sciences" has perhaps helped to focus interest on state behavior, on foreign policy, and on the processes of choice of decision-making elites.

(3) With the acceptance of the notion that somehow the world has changed, and world politics with it, in the era that has seen *inter alia* the passing of the European age, the rise of the super-powers, the Afro-Asian awakening, and the plural possession of thermonuclear weapons, the need is intensified for the observer to transcend his own time and culture and view them from some lofty point where the world politics of today can be seen as only one among a great variety of world political patterns that have been or could be. Otherwise, one can hardly grasp the significantly novel and the significantly familiar aspects of contemporary world politics.

---

in the theoretical efforts described above, as indeed they are in the body of literature conventionally called "political theory." Lasswell and Kaplan call only the first "theory" and describe the propounding of norms as "doctrine" (H. D. Lasswell and A. Kaplan, *Power and Society* (New Haven, 1950). Cf. Mortimer Adler, *How to Think About War and Peace* (New York, 1944). Adler uses "theory" similarly but contrasts it with "practice" which, he says, involves the introduction of ethical considerations.

The first and no doubt healthy response to the recognition that the European state system had become a world system and that the United States as a world power had world-wide concerns was that non-Western European area studies needed encouragement, not only the Soviet Union, the Far East and Latin America but more recently Africa, the Middle East and the rest of the Asian rimlands. Thus, the effort to be liberated from European culture-bound perspectives is far advanced and largely successful. But understanding the whole of world politics is a greater task, or at any rate a different one, than understanding the sum of its parts; and it is widely believed that theory can help us comprehend the whole.

The new interest in theory may be partly due to wholly unwarranted expectations regarding the kind of theoretical and doctrinal guidance which the scholar can offer the statesman or the thoughtfully responsible citizen. Some of the reputation for being able to work magic which the physical scientists won for themselves at Hiroshima may have rubbed off on the social scientist. He may in some cases come to believe that he too is or could be a wonder-worker. With some of the old sign-posts gone and some of those that remain evidently pointing the wrong way, he may be tempted to believe that he has been "called" to point the way, to believe there is a one-to-one relationship between his theory and the "right" foreign policy for his country or for the world.

IV

Whatever may be the "use" of the study of international relations, by which I understand whatever may be its impact on world politics and particularly on the behavior of states, it is not to relate big theory directly to big policy. Speculative activity can be no more useful than the subject which it illuminates.[6]

Theorizing can define the principles of exclusion and inclusion so that the distinctive task of the international relations scholar is differentiated from the tasks of social scientists in general. It can define the changing task of the investigator as it is modified by gross changes in world politics and in the state of the art of the investigator. Thus, technological and scientific change, formerly viewed as a long-run

---

6. On the task of the theorist in the social sciences generally, see Robert K. Merton, *Social Theory and Social Structure* (Glencoe, Ill., 1949).

variable, has in our generation come to be seen as a critical short-run variable; and technical possibilities for investigating the behavior of decision-making elites are making it possible to supplement traditional archival research with new methods for illuminating diplomatic behavior.

Theorizing also helps to define "important" subjects for investigation, i.e., important in terms of the investigators' value preferences. Arnold Wolfers' essay, "Political Theory and International Relations," has posed a very important question as to how much international relations thinking in Britain and America has been shaped by a philosophy of choice based on a real or imagined freedom of choice.[7] The present essay is perhaps an exemplification of such an attitude.

Theorizing ought to alert the investigator to limitations which are inherent in his mode of investigation. Is the baby being thrown out with the bath, for example, when one ignores the idiosyncratic behavior of individual states in order to discover certain laws about the behavior of states in general? How does one find a way of dealing with the unique as well as the recurring, of the particular as well as the general? Perhaps it depends on the question being asked, which of the two types of simplification of the real world is the more appropriate.

Any kind of rigor in scholarship requires that the ordering concepts be clarified. This theoretical activity has logically to precede data-collecting, although in actual research conceptual analysis is continually being stimulated by data which does not quite seem to fit. The verification or disverification of such a simple statement as that "All states seek to maximize their power positions" cannot proceed, for example, without defining and describing the "power" which is allegedly being maximized. Under one definition of power, the statement is hardly more than a tautology. Under another, power-seeking tends to be equated with all goal-oriented activity and thus may be that which differentiates animal from vegetable life, or at any rate, action from thought. With conceptual analysis, the significant question might be transformed from whether or not states seek to maximize power to what kind of power what groups seek to maximize under what conditions.

7. A. Wolfers and L. Martin, eds., *The Anglo-American Tradition in Foreign Affairs* (New Haven, 1956), pp. ix-xvii.

"National character" is another frequently ambiguous ordering concept. Are we talking about some *Volksgeist* or an objectively verifiable regularity in mass behavior or attitude which distinguishes one national group (or its influential elites) from some or all others? [8]

When we refer to a state's "national interest" are we talking about something objectively definable or are we in some way referring to a policy which would be rational if one posited such and such a value position?[9] If one assumed with Charles Beard, for example, that United States foreign policy was an expression of the interest of the group which happened to have captured control of the national government, then one would be positing that there were no national goals to be served via foreign policy and that the idea of national interest was a fraud.[10] It is worth noting that Charles Beard did have strong views that Franklin D. Roosevelt's foreign policy was contrary to America's (non-existent) national interest.

The significant question and the ordering concept need to be supplemented by the working model. This is a crude (or refined) approximation of the real world simplified by the fact that it seeks to answer only certain questions by using only certain kinds of data. It is only useful as it helps us to answer the question we are asking. There is no reason to suppose any one model of world politics will be more generally useful than all others, or for that matter more general than all others. To be told that states make war upon each other because man is a power-seeking animal by no means explains why there is sometimes war and sometimes peace, nor does it tell us why certain combinations of states have fought or may fight certain others. A theoretical statement, to be useful, has to be discriminating. It has to be general enough to apply to classes of cases, but not so general as to have no empirical referents whatever.

The apparent chaos of interstate relations in a multiple-sovereignty system can be "ordered" in a variety of ways by disciplined and disinterested observers. Some observers see regularities in the behavior of the states they are observing which permit them to theorize about

---

8. Cf. N. Leites, "Psycho-Cultural Hypotheses About Political Acts," *World Politics*, Vol. I, No. 1 (October 1948), pp. 102-119.
9. See a symposium exchange of views, H. J. Morgenthau and W. T. R. Fox, "National Interest and Moral Principles in Foreign Policy" in *The American Scholar*, Vol. 18, No. 2 (Spring 1949), pp. 207-216.
10. Cf. Charles A. Beard, *The Idea of National Interest* (New York, 1934).

the behavior of states in general, e.g., "All states seek to maximize their power positions." Others are able to explain the cycles of victory and defeat which various states have experienced in terms of key relationships, e.g., that between the "haves" and the "have nots" or that between "land power" and "sea power" or the struggle over some key area, the "Rimland," for example. Others leave questions of state motivation to one side and concern themselves solely with explanations for power differentials between states. No one of these approaches is more theoretical than another. None of them is necessarily incompatible with any other. What kind of abstraction is useful depends on the intellectual operation in which one is engaged.

Cartographers understand that no one flat map can be accurate as to more than one of the following: areas, directions, shapes. A globe sacrifices no two of these to the third, but it is incapable of showing detail and is of little use for navigation or geological surveys, for example. The analogy to international relations theory here suggested by cartography may be pertinent and exact.

No one theory may be equally accurate in explaining the cycle of peace and war, the rise and fall of great states, the extent to which the future is already implicit in the past, why certain states are "great powers," and so forth. A "global" theory which comprehended all these might not be of very much use in understanding, for example, how Western diplomacy has in our century sought to avoid having to deal with a Russo-German coalition. Theories of less architectonic proportions might be more useful in explaining this particular uniformity of state behavior, although of little use in some other context.

A theory which explains why States A, B, C. . . are strong and J, K, L. . . are not has its role, particularly if strength and/or weakness is really explained. While useful, it would have the same limited usefulness as the anthropologist's conception of a "pecking order" in indigenous cultures. It explains who has what — e.g., "status is measured by the number of cattle one owns" — but not who gets what, i.e., what qualities cause one's herd of cattle to grow and his fellow's to shrink. A conception of a pecking order in our state system is useful if one is seeking to explain the behavior of states in a state system at any given time or within a time period too short for the pecking order to be modified. It is useless to explain why the family of great powers changes, sometimes even without inter-great-power war. It is equally useless in explaining how a policy-maker can achieve for his state optimum security in an insecure world or how states generally can achieve an all-around increase in security.

It is idle to ask which model is best. Models, like concepts, need to be operationally defined and this depends on the prior identification of the significant operation — here again, "prior" in logic though not necessarily in time. A model which helped to make plausible the passing of the European age — as did, for example, Harold Sprout's analysis of the political consequences of nineteenth-century and twentieth-century improvements in overland transport[11] — might not be very useful in defining the conditions under which the super-powers could be expected to agree to arms limitation agreements in the field of manufacture, stockpiling, or delivery of nuclear weapons.

To be efficient, we have said, theories of international relations are necessarily partial; they are not equally useful for the answer of all questions. If only because they are partial, because they are only true *ceteris paribus,* one should hesitate before vaulting directly from theory to policy prescription. The greater the awareness and the more explicit the definition of "the other things being equal" qualification, the more efficient international relations theory can be in serving posited value positions, i.e., the more useful it can be as a rational guide to policy.

The study of international relationships may possibly, like modern physics, evolve toward the discovery of some inherent relationship among its ordering concepts of such elegant simplicity as Einstein's statement that energy is equal to mass multiplied by the square of the speed of light. But whether or not the student of international relations will ever attain a comparable level of general theoretical insight, he is not likely to be able to leap to that level of insight simply by closing the door of his study and speculating about power, the national interest, and the state of nature in world politics. And if, by any chance, a theorist today should stumble upon some simple, central truth about world politics which seems to explain a wide array of the phenomena of international politics, the chance is slight that he would be able to get general acceptance of either the correctness or the importance of the revolutionary new theoretical insight.

11. H. and M. Sprout, *Foundations of National Power* (Princeton, 1945).

In the meantime, let us be tolerant, even if sometimes skeptical, of each other's theories; as Mao-tse Tung has said, but apparently no longer believes: "Let all flowers bloom." We shall probably find it easier to agree that some of these flowers are weeds than that any one of the others is the fairest flower of all.

How shall we distinguish the weeds from the flowers? Let us call "weeds": (1) those theoretical statements that do not purport to answer questions we regard as important or relevant; (2) those whose ordering concepts have no clear empirical referents or ones so ambiguous that they are incapable of verification or disverification, much less proof; (3) those which create a model of world politics which is such a distortion of reality that it obfuscates rather than clarifies when one tries to relate the imagined world to the observed one; (4) those that fail to take account of variables important to the answering of the question being asked; (5) those with more variables than are essential to give an equally accurate answer; (6) those that turn out on analysis to be tautological; (7) those that conceal within themselves assumptions of which their author is not fully aware; (8) those that are parochial because their author has presented them as transcendent but has failed to transcend his own time, or class, or ethnic affiliation; (9) those that are internally inconsistent; (10) those with unambiguous empirical referents whose behavior is inconsistent with the theory; (11) those that confuse statements of fact and of preference; (12) those which are *post factum* and topical; (13) those that prescribe for the world as if it were a clean slate on which anything could be written.[12]

V

The relationship between theory and policy is two-way, complex and sometimes indirect. One of the reasons, we have said, why a

---

12. Weeds in the flower garden of theory are often found where the earth is richest, and what is one man's flower may be another man's weed. J. U. Nef, *War and Human Progress* (Cambridge, Mass., 1950), is a work of first-rate importance for anyone speculating about technology and international relations, although the question the author seeks to answer, "Does war contribute to human progress?" is not one which an international relations theorist would be likely to ask; nor is Professor Nef's answer one which is of either descriptive or prescriptive significance with respect to the decisions of leaders of national governments to embark upon or refrain from embarking upon particular wars.

given problem may be regarded as "significant" or worth working on is that its solution is regarded as important to promoting or maintaining certain values. But the significant problem may seem to defy solution if attacked directly. Intensive search for the cure for the war disease may take place quite far from the site of the war epidemic, and this in turn may beckon the investigator on to new explorations whose relation to the original problem is only dimly perceived if it is even considered at all. It may often happen that the solution to a problem comes while one is working on quite a different problem. But without a theoretical framework one might miss the key insight which one "accidentally" discovers.

For the relationship of theory to policy to be one-way, simple and direct, several conditions would have to be met. Theory would have to be a pyramidal, symmetrical structure of ideas whose highest point encompassed all the wisdom of the lower levels. The theorist and the policy-makers would have to be in perfect understanding as to the values being promoted. Finally, the theory would have to provide the discriminating basis for choice among all policy alternatives, major and minor, without the addition of either further theories or further facts.

With or without a theory of international relations, the findings of modern social science will be utilized in an era of efficient public administration and protracted high-level mobilization in much the same way that any other community resource will be utilized. If sociologists can demonstrate how friction can be alleviated between personnel in large military installations and the population of neighboring cities, they may make members of the armed forces abroad more efficient instruments of national policy. If social psychologists can illuminate the theory of small-group behavior, there may be some useful clues as to how American negotiators ought to behave in specified international conference situations. This *ad hoc* utilization for the more efficient conduct of foreign relations of this or that research finding differs, however, in no important respect from the way in which any large-scale enterprise, private or public, would utilize it. There is no theoretical problem raised by the addition of such insights on a piecemeal basis to the intellectual capital of the student of world politics or the practitioner of diplomacy.

One can therefore eliminate in advance one type of question from the agenda of theory, viz.: "What is the nature of the general contribution to international relations which sociology (or psychology or anthropology or statistics or geography or history or what have you) makes?" The answer is that sociology (psychology, etc.) in general, does not contribute to international relations in general. Specific sociological (psychological, etc.) insights may provide practical and sometimes direct assistance to the policy-maker. They also become, like other records of human action, data of possible relevance to the international relations theorist. No overarching theory is, however, required for a diplomatist to make use of a report that in certain cultures it is conventional to grin when reporting a personal tragedy; and it is difficult to see how such a report would be of any direct use to the theorist, however helpful it might be to a diplomat on a specific occasion.

Let us consider, however, some other contributions of the non-political sciences. The accumulation of evidence that differences in skin pigmentation and all other physical differences which are conventionally associated with "race" correlate in no significant way with innate intellectual capacity, has evidently had a powerful effect on theories of international relations which presupposed permanently unequal relations between political groupings of Western European culture and what were widely believed to be lesser breeds in God's scheme of things. The accumulating evidence that man typically strives to maximize a multiplicity of values serves to warn those who may create theoretical models based on some simplistic assumption that men or groups of men subordinate their every action to the maximization of some one value — material gain, power, self-respect, etc.[13] Theorists, in general, and single-value systematizers in particular, may not legitimately prescribe for the ills of the real world without taking full account of the simplifications which, knowingly or unknowingly, they introduce into their theoretical model. Social science can be a corrective both to Marx and to Machiavelli, as well as to those who would follow them in too slavish a fashion.

The data on race and on value-maximization have something in

13. See H. D. Lasswell, "The Normative Impact of the Behavioral Sciences," *Ethics,* Vol. LXVII, No. 3 (April 1957), Part II.

common which distinguishes them from the earlier cited examples of the direct *ad hoc* application of one particular finding of social science to one particular form of social action — the conduct of foreign relations. Their impact on foreign policy and on world politics generally is indirect. In each case the new data has affected scholars' images of world politics. These modifications in theoretical perspective in time are diffused "up" to policy-making levels which are more immediately influential.

This type of contribution to the continuing reconstruction of the scholar's image of world politics can be made on the initiative of the scholar himself, provided he has the curiosity to keep abreast of advances in the behavioral sciences and to ask questions of his non-international relations colleagues which he alone can ask and they alone can answer. It can also be made on the initiative of the non-international relations behavioral scientist, provided his knowledge of the matrix of thinking about world politics is sufficient to enable him to know what kinds of questions the international relations scholar would ask if he knew the data existed, or could be made to exist, to answer those questions.

This is the kind of contribution which can lead to complications and refinements of the theoretician's model of world politics. The complexity however may become so great that the model comes to resemble a Rube Goldberg apparatus. The intellectual output may be somewhat less than its input unless there is selective simplification of the model in the light of both the question being asked and the latest relevant findings of the behavioral sciences.

Simplification may sometimes flow from ignorance and even from a willful determination to ignore inconvenient data, but a scholar's simplification is deliberate. Suppose it is true that power is sought most frequently as a means of achieving non-power ends, but suppose it generally turns out, within the context of the international relations question being investigated, that power is regarded as the sole reliable means to achieve the other "higher" (i.e., more socially acceptable) ends. Note, however, the qualification, "suppose it generally turns out. ..." If research should show, for example, that it was something called "security" rather than something called "power" towards which at least some states moved, say the rich and fat ones, or the insular ones, or those which could have no real hope of ever being top rooster in the international pecking order, the model might have to be modified. Or suppose analysis should show that all the hard choices which a government had to make in foreign and military policy related not to the question whether to seek power but rather to the question: "What kind and how much shall we mobilize to meet which combination of threats during what time periods?" Then the model, at least for short-term analysis, would have to be reconsidered.

In the absence of data, a theoretical model tends to be simple. New data must, initially at least, complicate the model, although as relationships become clearer and correlations closer the number of genuinely independent variables to be handled may ultimately decrease.

More typically, we have said, models are simplified "operationally." If one's concern is to establish the limits within which the family of great powers is to be expected to vary over the next half century — this would have been a very useful exercise a century or so ago, and De Tocqueville and List did predict the emergence of the great Russian and American super-powers — one can immediately exclude all kinds of data relevant to the answer of other equally important international relations questions. To summarize, ignorant and unavoidable simplifications of reality reduce the relevance of theory to policy, while operational simplifications enhance its relevance.

Theory operates, however indirectly, to modify the attitudes and beliefs both of a government's supporters and of its potential effective critics. In both cases, greater theoretical insight acts to increase the rationality of choice of the policy-maker. Through theoretical investigations certain goals are seen to be unreal or unattainable or inconsistent with other "higher" goals or more costly than previously imagined. Other goals may come to be seen as more possible than was once generally believed. Thus, the theorist not only heightens the rationality of the decision-maker's choices, but he provides the decision-maker with the basis for reformulating his value position.

VI

The future is not a *tabula rasa* on which we are free to write what we choose. But neither are we puppets dancing on the stage of history in response to "first causes," "basic factors," or, for that matter, inevitable progress toward bringing the Kingdom of God down on this earth. Rational political action consists in achieving the best possible reconciliation of the desirable and the possible.

We ought therefore to attempt to order the blooming, buzzing confusion of world politics by collecting and arranging our data so that it helps us to understand the relatively fixed, the changing but uncontrollable, and manipulatable aspects of world politics. Within the range of the changeable, we need to collect data which help us to predict ever more accurately the consequences of particular courses of action.

If man is to have the opportunity to exercise some measure of rational control over his destiny, the limits of the possible and the consequences of the desirable have both to be investigated. A theory of international relations is thus needed which distinguishes:

a) the "givens" in the world political equation — e.g., resources, shapes of continents, conception of politics as an unending process (however its form may change);
b) long-run basic changes — e.g., rise of nationalism, spread of coal-and-iron technology, the demographic revolution;
c) the policies of other states over which one's own state has relatively slight control and the policies of one's own state which are not chosen primarily in a foreign policy context;
d) the remaining area of choice — e.g., levels of preparedness; patterns of alliance; use of organization to adjust conflict or facilitate peaceful change.

Whether one views world politics from the desk of a great-power foreign minister at a critical moment of choice or from the desk of a scholar in a university during an inter-crisis period of peace, there must almost inevitably be a restless search for the variables in the situation which one can modify and which, if modified, would result in a more efficient protection or promotion of whatever the viewer, whether policy-maker or theorist, regards as valuable. Each seeks to bring about a reconciliation of the desirable and the possible along lines more satisfactory than had hitherto seemed feasible to him.

Not all of the factors which the theorist must in proper humility — writing away from the seat of government, outside the domain of official secrecy and before the event — label as an area of choice, will be seen as such by the man on the inside at the moment of choice. The maker of policy also lacks perfect knowledge, however much his areas of ignorance may have been narrowed by general theoretical understanding or specific official intelligence. His choices lack the clarity which historians and social scientists, after the event and with their bias toward orderly explanations, impose on his action. But it is his sense of the deficiency of the theoretical and practical guidance available to him at moments of difficult choice which is one source in the formulation of new "problems" and the restarting of the policy-theory-policy cycle of interaction.

The theorist's quest for precise definition and imaginative expansion of the range of future choice should lead him to focus neither on the absolutely invariant nor on the inherently unknowable or the completely uncontrollable. The realms of the wholly fixed or wholly predictable and the wholly uncontrollable need to be defined, but the energies of research and theory ought to concentrate on that which lies in between.

The shape of the continents is fixed and so is the distribution of natural resources under the earth's crust. The atom has been split and nuclear weapons can hardly be "un-invented," except under circumstances that would make theorizing about future politics irrelevant.

Population growth rates are changing and changing at different rates. Whether or not governments can significantly affect differentials in growth rates, they are hardly likely to do so in a foreign policy context. Here too is a type of "given" which has to be set down and kept in mind, a dynamic factor which cannot be manipulated either in the Foreign Office or in the study of the international relations scholar.

Ideas and attitudes are perhaps more subject to deliberate modification, although the scholar and the artificer of foreign policy have no long-run monopoly in manipulating thought and not much possibility of significantly influencing it at all in the short-run.[14] Nationalism as a force runs deep, and its recent development in Africa and Asia could probably not have been thwarted by any policy whatever.

---

14. In the short run a selective presentation of "facts" can, of course, gain for the policy-maker some immediate freedom of maneuver.

Its impact on policy in Europe and North America, however, can surely be modified by theoretical discussion of the North Atlantic community, of Western European integration, and of Western relations with the ex-colonial areas.

The United States government cannot by any particular foreign policy relieve the population pressure in India or raise Chinese living standards to equal American standards. But if it has greater understanding than it now does of the specific political consequences of various forms of military, economic and technical assistance and of alternative psychological strategies, it can minimize some of the undesired consequences of the prevailing inequality in living standards.

United States diplomacy cannot by applying what is known about the behavior of diplomatists within the Western European culture area operate with maximum efficiency in other culture areas, but the promotion of area studies can help close this particular gap.

Wishing will not make super-powers of the former European great powers; but an analysis of the political consequences of varying degrees of West European integration reveals, as an ultimate possibility, the creation of a single West European super-power. It thus clarifies discussion in a genuine area of choice.

Analysis of the changed significance of power potential in an era in which a new world war might be very short, can highlight the critical nature of government decisions regarding the defense budget.

Neither side can compel arms limitation agreements, but the conditions under which restrictions on nuclear arms would make both sides feel more secure can be clarified by stating the problem with theoretical rigor.

The former colonial and semi-colonial populations can hardly be made to love those whom they only recently regarded as exploiters, but this does not mean that the actions of Western states make no difference or that one course of action will not serve a given value position much better than another.

In a longer time perspective, it may be that some of the features of our state system which have been regarded as invariant — the balance of power and national self-determination as both expectations and norms; total war as a feasible policy alternative, etc. — may turn out to be characteristic only of our state system in a particular stage of its evolution. What are the range of alternative futures which the theorist can envision? These must be systematically described before those in and out of government whose opinions determine policy can rationally select policy.

The key words in this analysis have been "theory," "doctrine," and "policy." Theory is useful because it organizes social science so as, marginally at least, to heighten the rationality of choice, official and unofficial. It does not do this directly; it does it by clarifying doctrinal positions, by pointing to the most efficient means to move toward desired ends, and by minimizing the area of contingency and sheer ignorance which the policy-maker can never hope completely to eliminate. More specifically, theory can focus research on what might be called the quasi-contingent, the factors that are neither absolutely invariant or uncontrollable nor absolutely unknown or unpredictable.

VII

The vocation of leadership is a stern one, and a scholar is not solely by virtue of his scholarly attributes equipped to lead. Politics, as Max Weber wrote in another time of trouble, "is the slow boring of hard boards." This observation applies also to international politics. The moral imperative is no less, it is indeed greater, and the task is arduous. The social scientist must be aware both of his potentialities and his limitations *as a social scientist* if he is to perform his distinctive function, but he need be no moral eunuch to perform that function. He must never forget that as a social scientist he is not called upon to tell men what they ought to want. If international politics is the slow boring of hard boards, it is not the social scientist's task either to assert that the boards are in fact soft or to say where the holes ought to be bored. It is his task to say where the knots are likely to be if he knows, and what consequences may properly be expected if boring takes place here rather than there, and to provide as sharp tools as possible for the boring. To perform this task he needs to construct a frame in which systematic and imaginative hypothesizing most readily occurs. In other words, he must make use of theory.

Chapter IV

POLITICAL PHILOSOPHY AND THE STUDY OF INTERNATIONAL RELATIONS[1]

BY KENNETH N. WALTZ

THE STUDY of traditional political philosophy has been neglected more by teachers and students of international relations than by political scientists who are concerned primarily with American and comparative government. There is mounting evidence that it may not remain so for long. Increasingly one finds expression given to the conviction that continuing disregard of formal theory, whether in policy making or in research, is to be deplored. Among men of affairs, the Labour M.P. Denis Healey writes that his Party has too often fallen victim to "utopianism" because as a whole it "lacks any systematic theory of world affairs. . . ."[2] Though a non-partisan observer might say, less charitably, that the Party's theory while more systematic than most was simply wrong, Healey in his essay nevertheless underscores the importance of theory in the practical realm of Party policy. On this side of the Atlantic, Dean Acheson, who is not on record while Secretary of State as sensing an urgent need for highly abstract analyses of international relations, now pleads with some urgency and argues with considerable eloquence the need for precisely such activity.[3] One could easily multiply the number of examples and

1. This essay is a slightly revised version of a paper read at the fifty-third annual meeting of the American Political Science Association in New York City, September, 1957.
2. Denis Healey, "Power Politics and the Labour Party," R. H. S. Crossman, ed., *New Fabian Essays* (London, 1952), pp. 161-162.
3. See his introduction to Louis J. Halle, *Civilization and Foreign Policy* (New York, 1955).

more easily still add to them a list of scholarly studies that reflect a deepening concern with international relations theory.

Yet testimonials to the importance of theory, however eloquent, do not themselves establish the usefulness of the political philosophy of the past. A high regard for systematic theory is often coupled with disdain for traditional political philosophy. The question remains: What if anything can present-day students of international relations learn from perusing classical works in political philosophy? The purpose of this essay is to examine two of the possible claims of political philosophers upon the attention of students of international relations. We shall briefly consider the writings of political philosophers as a source of aid in dealing with current problems; at greater length, we shall discuss the importance of general theory in the study of international relations and the uses of political philosophy in working out such a theory.

The political scientist concerned with problems of coalition warfare will clearly profit from familiarity with the history of the Napoleonic wars. The play of mind over historical matter will suggest patterns, parallels with more recent events, pitfalls to be avoided, hypotheses to be considered. The political scientist concerned with civil-military relations will gain a variety of insights from contemplating the cases of Bismarck, of his immediate successors, of the German generals under Hitler. In similar fashion one may argue that for the study of many problems there are clues to be gained from a long and thoughtful look at the writings of political philosophers. In Plato and Aristotle, for example, in Machiavelli and Hobbes, in Adam Smith and Friedrich Engels, from the earliest to the most recent Western political philosophers one finds the problem of civilian control of the military and of the effects of military organization and personnel on constitutions and governance identified and commented upon as matters of some importance. No argument is required to establish the thought that speculations of eminent minds on matters of abiding importance have some relevance today. Yet one can scarcely build an impressive case for the study of political philosophy on these grounds. Even were I to summarize here the materials just mentioned, I could say little to the retort that, while on these problems Hobbes had something of interest to say, one can learn much more from a comparative study of British and German institutions and practices, from an historical study of American institutions, or from any of a number of other approaches. On this level, the argument for the study of political philosophy is the same as the argument that one profits from knowing some history, that knowledge and ideas may be picked up from Thucydides and Ranke, or, for that matter, from Aristophanes and Shakespeare. There are modest and immediately practical ideas to be found in political philosophy, and they are too often overlooked, but it properly remains with the person who is teaching or doing research to decide which materials will be most helpful. It would be foolhardy to press this particular claim of the political philosophers too far.

Though the first claim of the political philosophers upon our attention is notably weak, the second is not. The interests that the student reflects in his studies most often reflect in turn his estimate of the day's most pressing problems. His manner of approaching these problems most often embodies the currently most popular methodology, however vaguely grounded and sketchily elaborated. The pragmatic and fluctuating character of work in the field of international relations attests to these facts. In this century, teachers and students have shifted their concentration first from international law and the workings of the Peace Movement to diplomatic history and international organization, and then from the composition and uses of power to the decision-making processes. The changing focus of interest has paralleled changes in events. There is not necessarily anything wrong with this. What is disturbing, however, is the lack of self-criticism among those who have adopted a particular approach and more disturbing still the extent to which the problem of systematically interrelating different approaches has been neglected.

Whether our interest be how to avoid a war and how to win one if avoidance is impossible or, conceivably, how to make a war possible at a time that it can be won, we are all in one way or another concerned with the causes of war and the conditions of peace, whichever of various approaches may claim our major attention. This continuing concern opens the way to a critical, theoretical examination of the relevance of different approaches to the study of the factors making for war or peace.

But what rewards can such a theoretical study promise? Whatever the putative gains, one may argue that historical studies, bypassing often intricate theoretical problems, promise gains still larger. Why not, for example, study past wars, figure out their causes and ask ourselves what can be done to eliminate them or restrict their operation in the future? Or why not look directly at points of tension in the world and investigate them empirically in order to devise means of alleviation? Such approaches are often used. On the basis of the latter type of study Warren S. Thompson warned in the 1920's that the countries of the world suffering from the pressure of population upon resources would wage war to solve their problems unless the "have" countries shared their riches of land with the "have nots." [4] His estimate of cause seems to be stated in a form that permits empirical-historical testing. On closer inspection, however, a number of difficulties becomes apparent. Clearly, different population pressures, even where the differences are large and greatly to the disadvantage of some states, do not always produce wars. It becomes impossible to estimate the significance, or insignificance, of this one factor without relating it to others. But what are the other factors and how great is the importance of each of them?

In order to make sense of the hypothesis we need somehow to acquire an idea of the interrelation of many possibly relevant factors, and these interrelations are not given in the data. We establish or, rather, assert them ourselves. To say "establish" would be dangerous, for descriptive statements and statements of cause are of two different orders. Empirically one can demonstrate that a given statement is not silly, that there is some basis in fact for it. This, however, is seldom conclusive; often it is not compelling. One may find a high correlation between variations in rainfall in Afghanistan and in the suicide rate in New York City. No one would thereupon assume a causal relation between the two sets of figures. To do so would be to insult common sense. But just what does the phrase "to insult common sense" mean? It means that there is no elaborated and accepted system by which a statement of interconnection becomes plausible.

Stating these points may make them seem obvious, yet they are often overlooked. They constitute not merely a justification for theory

4. Warren S. Thompson, *Danger Spots in World Population* (New York, 1929).

but an argument that theorizing is an omnipresent, though often merely implicit, operation. As a simple illustration, consider the following statement from an article written by a Chinese Communist. Having referred to the friendship and cooperation that exists "where states reflect the will of the people," as do China and the Soviet Union, the author inquires into the causes of tensions elsewhere in the world. She finds them in the interests and activities of men like Charles Wilson who, "being both the chief manufacturer of war materials for the United States government and its Secretary of Defense, says: 'What is good for my business is good for the country.'" Such men feed and grow fat on the enmity among peoples that they have themselves produced.[5] Factually much of her statement is substantially though not literally accurate. Wilson was at the time Secretary of Defense, he had been president of a large corporation, that corporation has supplied a large amount of war material to the United States armed forces, and he did make a comment somewhat similar to the one she attributes to him. The element of factual accuracy in the statement does not, however, make it plausible to me. Nor is it factual accuracy that makes the statement plausible to a communist. The "facts" she relates simply supply evidence for a belief already entertained. The belief consists of a picture of the world, an understanding of the causal connections among events, in short an elaborated system that gives meaning to data otherwise unrelated. Is the elaborated system, in this case the Marxist explanation of the causes of war, an accurate one? No amount of data collecting can prove it so, for data do not interpret themselves. The facts may seem to support a given theory; they may support a radically different theory still better.

Accepting this argument, one may conclude that it supports the contention that in his work the social scientist, unlike the natural scientist, is unavoidably subjective. Yet the same difficulties plague and must continue to plague the natural scientist. A brief examination of this proposition will serve to make clearer the role of theory and the limits of empiricism in all inquiry.

The Ptolemaic system was accepted for centuries and a multitude of observations confirmed its scientific adequacy. In the sixteenth cen-

5. Song Ching Ling, "Friendship of the Peoples and Peace," *China Reconstructs* (Peking), January-February, 1954, pp. 2-4.

tury Copernicus, unaware that he was reviving an earlier hypothesis of Aristarchus, advanced a radically different theory. His reason for doing so was more a dissatisfaction with the aesthetically unpleasing complexity of the Ptolemaic system than it was the difficulty of fitting increasing amounts of data into the then commonly accepted theoretical structure. E. A. Burtt, a modern philosopher of science, says flatly that there were at the time of Copernicus "no known celestial phenomena which were not accounted for by the Ptolemaic method with as great accuracy as could be expected without more modern instruments. Predictions of astronomical events were made which varied no more from the actual occurrence than did predictions made by a Copernican. . . . in this case there was distinctly no gain in accuracy." He adds that "Contemporary empiricists, had they lived in the sixteenth century, would have been first to scoff out of court the new philosophy of the universe." [6]

Francis Bacon, the seventeenth-century prophet of empiricism, attacked the metaphysics of Aristotle and opposed the assumption of *a priori* certainty wherever he found it, though this meant ridiculing the methods and accomplishments of Kepler, Galileo, and Gilbert. Newton, influenced by both the deductive mathematical and the inductive experimental schools, came more and more to proclaim himself an apostle of the second. "Whatever is not deduced from the phenomena," he wrote in the *Principia*, "is to be called an hypothesis; and hypotheses, whether metaphysical or physical, whether of occult qualities or mechanical, have no place in experimental philosophy. In this philosophy particular propositions are inferred from the phenomena, and afterwards rendered general by induction." [7] Knowledge of the world about us is to be seized directly by an inductive method that as rigorously excludes *ad hoc* hypotheses as it does grandiose metaphysics. But did Newton escape metaphysics or, in trying to escape, did he merely accept uncritically the metaphysical assumptions of his age? Burtt argues that he did the latter. To the question, what is real, he replied in effect, that to which my method can be applied. To the

---

6. Edwin Arthur Burtt, *The Metaphysical Foundations of Modern Physical Science* (Garden City, N.Y., 1954), pp. 36, 38. The book was first published in 1924; a revised edition appeared in 1932.
7. *Ibid.*, p. 218.

question, how can one obtain a knowledge of the whole, he replied, by studying its parts.

Laplace hailed Newton not as the genius of his age but as the genius of all past and future time. He had discovered the laws of the universe, which, like America, can only be discovered once. But discovery, in science as in geography, is partly a matter of acceptance. And, as Hume so well argued, it is a logical error to assume that certainty can be produced by piling up experimental data. It is tempting to believe that explication can be undertaken without philosophic assumptions and to believe further that a multitude of experiments confirming a given proposition can produce certainty. Yet Newton's system, though it fostered magnificent scientific and technological accomplishments, though its major propositions were tested and proved over a period of centuries, now appears as but a special case of a more general system.

The preceding discussion emphasizes the role of theory, of assumptions and preconceptions. This is not to decry the empirical testing of theories and hypotheses but rather to convey the thought that the frequently heard plea for more hypotheses in testable form, and for more theories so constructed that testable hypotheses can be derived from them, should always be accompanied by a warning. Empirical verification, while important, cannot produce certainty, in the social or in the natural sciences, for by the most intricate and oft-repeated tests one does not exclude alternative possibilities. The tests are conclusive only with reference to the assumptions postulated. There is then not only the necessity of checking theory against facts but also the necessity of checking one theory against others. To establish the credibility of a proposition, logical-analytic as well as empirical operations are required. Secondly, to sum up Burtt's criticism of Newton in the simpler language of Alfred North Whitehead, "Induction presupposes metaphysics." [8] The second point is intimately related to the first.

8. Alfred North Whitehead, *Science and the Modern World* (New York, 1925, reprint of 1948), p. 65. The rest of the passage is worth quoting. "In other words, it [induction] rests upon an antecedent rationalism. You cannot have a rational justification for your appeal to history till your metaphysics has assured you that there *is* a history to appeal to; and likewise your conjectures as to the future presuppose some basis of knowledge that there *is* a future already subjected to some determinations. The difficulty is to make sense of either of these ideas. But unless you have done so, you have made nonsense of induction."

Robert Merton, for example, has asserted that "systematic sociological theory... represents the highly selective accumulation of those small parts of earlier theory which have thus far survived the test of empirical research." [9] Proceeding in this manner one may, no doubt, produce systematic theory. The theory, of course, may turn out to be analogous to the Ptolemaic theory, systematically constructed, with its eighty-odd equations empirically tested and forming a schema able to explain the phenomena at hand. The difficulty is built in, not accidental, and the clue to it is given in the word "selective." Selected, one must ask, according to what principle? Empiricists have come to admit that their researches proceed from hypotheses. Hypotheses, Professor Merton avers, are best derived from "theories of the middle range." And how does one formulate the middle-range theories? Apparently this is done by drawing inferences from and logically interrelating propositions of still smaller size, for the immaturity of the social as compared to the physical sciences does not permit social scientists "to deal fruitfully with abstractions of a high order...." [10] We must build *toward* the higher order of abstraction. This overlooks the fact that many of the greatest natural scientists, even in the nonage of their disciplines, built *upon* highly abstract and truly breathtaking generalizations.

In a recent article, the physicist John Rader Platt concludes that "the pressure of scientific determinism becomes weak and random as we approach the great unitary syntheses. For they are not only discoveries. They are also artistic creations, shaped by the taste and style of a single hand." [11] The effect of the idea, and of the mode and method of inquiry, is far-reaching; and submerging the idea, allowing it to remain implicit, makes the statement no less true. Whitehead points up the materialist predilections of modern science, rooted in a set of assumptions both fructifying and self-denying. The Copernican-Galilean-Newtonian image of the world focused scientists' atten-

---

9. Robert K. Merton, *Social Theory and Social Structure* (Glencoe, Ill., 1949), p. 5. The point is often made. I focus on Professor Merton's formulation since it is the most thoughtful and perceptive one I know of. His indicated awareness of some of the points made here (cf. especially *ibid.*, pp. 9-10, 85-86), however, makes more puzzling his one-sided emphasis on "theories of the middle range."
10. *Ibid.*, p. 84.
11. John Rader Platt, "Style in Science," *Harper's Magazine,* October 1956, p. 75.

tion on motion and matter and fostered an advance in physics at the expense of first neglecting and then introducing a bias into the study of chemistry and biology.[12]

In social and political affairs, one finds equally impressive examples of the far-reaching effects of central ideas, implicitly or explicitly held. Some events and conditions must be explained in terms of others. Often of decisive importance in the explanation is the answer to the question, where does the explanation begin? In accounting for the recurrence of war, for example, liberals and socialists have markedly inclined to an inside-out explanation. The behavior of states varies with their internal structure — political, economic, and social. In the liberal formulation, despotism is warlike and democracy is the uniquely peaceful form of the state. This formulation has, however, been controverted as often as it has been advanced. Herodotus observed that it is comparatively easy to persuade a multitude to foolish military adventure, and the same observation was made by both Aristophanes and Thucydides.[13] Ever since, similar refutation has been undertaken whenever circumstances have made it relevant. But historical refutation is seldom accepted as conclusive. In 1953 *The New York Times* argued editorially that "No true democracy. . . can be aggressive. Aggression begins at home. No free majority will ever vote for it."[14] If a democracy does initiate a war, one can always define it as preventive rather than aggressive. Failing this, one can always argue that the supposedly free majority that supported it was not in fact free enough.

As significant, however, as the attempt to sustain or demolish the proposition in empirical or scholastic fashion is the effort to establish an opposing causal perspective by starting the explanation at a different point. It has, for example, often been argued that the formula "democracies are peaceful; autocracies are warlike" reverses the causation. It is in this view not the internal structures of states that determine questions of war and peace, but questions of war and peace that, sometimes at least, determine the constitutions of states. This is

---

12. Whitehead, *op. cit.*, especially chs. v, vi.
13. *The History of Herodotus*, tr. George Rawlinson (Everyman's Library; London, 1949), II, 46, 110. Aristophanes, *The Knights, The Acharnians,* and *Peace*. Thucydides, tr. B. Jowett (2nd ed.; London, 1900), Bk. VI, par. 18.
14. March 23, 1953, p. 22.

the thesis that Leopold Ranke derived from, or applied to, the history of the states of modern Europe.[15] The same thesis has been used to explain, in part or in entirety, the structure of other constitutions.[16]

Most English liberals at the time of the First World War argued that the militarist and authoritarian character of the German state prompted Germany to seek the war that soon embroiled most of the world. At the same time some liberals, most notably G. Lowes Dickinson, argued that no single state could be held guilty. Only by understanding the international system, or lack of system, by which the leaders of states were often forced to act with slight regard for conventional morality, could one understand and justly assess the processes by which the war came about.[17] Dickinson was blasted by liberals and socialists alike for reversing the dominant inside-out explanation. Acceptance or rejection of explanatory theses in matters such as this most often depends on the skill of the pleaders and the mood of the audience. These are obviously not fit criteria, yet it would be foolish to argue that simply by taking a more intensive look at the data one can build a compelling case for one or the other explanatory theory. Staring at the same set of data, the parties to the debate came to sharply different conclusions, for the images they entertained led them to select and interpret the data in different ways. The estimate of cause is an idea related to but not identical with the occurrence one seeks to explain. The idea we entertain becomes a filter through which we pass our data. If the filter is good or the data selected carefully, they will pass like milk through cheesecloth. The recalcitrance of the data may cause us to change one filter for another, to modify or scrap the theory we hold — or it may produce ever more ingenious selections and interpretations of the data, as has happened with many Marxists trying to salvage the thesis that with the development of capitalism the masses become increasingly impoverished.

If empirical investigations vary in incidence and result with the ideas the empiricists entertain, it is worth asking ourselves if the ideas themselves can be subjected to scrutiny. Obviously they can be. It is

---

15. "The Great Powers," tr. H. H. von Laue, in Theodore H. von Laue, *Leopold Ranke, The Formative Years* (Princeton, 1950).
16. See, for example, Leon Homo, *Roman Political Institutions,* tr. M. R. Dobie (London, 1929), especially pp. 146, 364-369.
17. G. Lowes Dickinson, *The European Anarchy* (New York, 1917).

at this point that political philosophy can make its major contribution. The study of politics is distinguished from other social studies by concentration upon the institutions and processes of government. This focuses the political scientists' concern without constituting a self-denying ordinance against the use of materials and techniques of other social scientists.[18] On the latter point there is no difficulty for the student of international relations; there is considerable difficulty on the former, for international relations are characterized by the absence of truly governmental institutions, which in turn gives a radically different twist to the relevant processes. Yet there is a large and important sense in which traditional political philosophy, concentrating as it does upon domestic politics, is relevant for the student of international relations. Peace, it is often said, is the problem of the twentieth century. It is, as well, one of the continuing concerns of political philosophers. In times of relative quiescence the question men put is likely to be: What good is life without justice and freedom? Better to die than live a slave. In times of domestic troubles, of hunger and civil war, of pressing insecurity, however, many will ask: Of what use is freedom without a power sufficient to establish and maintain conditions of security? That life takes priority over justice and freedom is taken to be a self-evident truth by St. Augustine and Luther, by Machiavelli, Bodin, and Hobbes. If the alternative to tyranny is chaos and if chaos means a war of all against all, then the willingness to endure tyranny becomes understandable. In the absence of order there can be no enjoyment of liberty. The problem of identifying and achieving the conditions of peace, a problem that plagues man and bedevils the student of international relations has, especially in periods of crisis, bedeviled political philosophers as well.

Concern with the conditions of stability and peace necessitates in turn concern with the causes of disorder, including the most dramatic disorder, war. This may be called the theodicy problem translated into secular terms: man's explanation to himself of the existence of evil. The late R. G. Collingwood suggested that the most direct route to understanding the writings of philosophers is to seek out the ques-

---

18. Cf. David B. Truman, "The Impact on Political Science of the Revolution in the Behavioral Sciences," *Research Frontiers in Politics and Government* (Washington, D.C., 1955), pp. 202-231.

tions they were attempting to answer. I would suggest that posing a central question and ordering systematically the different answers that can be given to it is the most direct route to the construction of international-political theory. I would argue further that in attempting to construct such a theory one can profit greatly from a close familiarity with the works of those commonly regarded as major figures in the history of political philosophy. If, as I have suggested above, we cannot escape from philosophy, then to ignore the political philosophy of the past is to proceed on the hubristic assumption that each person can and should be his own political philosopher. Aside from the difficulties posed by differences in capabilities and temperaments, this attitude makes for a great repetition of work already done.

Yet one must admit that answers given by political philosophers to the question as to why wars recur, are bewildering in their variety and contradictory qualities. One who looks at the elaborated systems of political philosophers sees a number of pictures painted by artists who highlight different "realities." What in the picture is substance, what is shadow? Which elements exist in the world around us, which merely in the artists' eyes? Even to attempt to answer such questions, the variety of interpretations has to be ordered in such a way as to make it manageable. In the interest of brevity, I can here merely say, with the briefest of substantive comments, that re-examining political philosophy with an eye open to the questions just posed leads one, or at least has led me, to the conclusion that under the following three categories the variety can be ordered without artificially reducing it, thus facilitating comparison and critical evaluation. Though painfully aware of the dangers of treating the corpus of political philosophy so eclectically, I think it necessary to do so since it is frustrating to read an argument that political philosophy has contributions to make without at least a hint of what these contributions may be. The following comments are not intended to establish the thought that there is a single way to use political philosophy in the study of international relations but merely to summarize, by way of example, an application that the author has personally found helpful.[19]

According to one view of international relations, the locus of the

19. The categories here set forth are developed more fully in Kenneth N. Waltz, *Man, the State, and War* (in press, New York, 1959).

major causes of war is found in the nature and behavior of man. Wars, according to this image of the world, result from selfishness, from misdirected aggressive impulses, from stupidity, from lack of information; other causes are secondary and have to be interpreted in the light of these factors. If these are the primary causes of war, then an end to war must come through uplifting and enlightening men or securing their psychic-social readjustment. This estimate of causes and possible cures has been dominant in the writings of many serious students of human affairs from Confucius to present-day pacifists. It is the leitmotif of many modern-day behavioral scientists as well. Clyde Kluckhohn, to cite one example from the many available, has identified "the central problem of world peace" as one of minimizing and controlling "aggressive impulses." [20] W. Fred Cottrell, to cite another, defines the presently remaining prerequisite for peace as "a clear understanding on the part of all elites that war is inferior to peace in pursuit of their values." [21] One may, however, agree with the first-image analysis of causes without admitting the possibility of meaningful prescription for their removal. St. Augustine attributes to man's love for "so many vain and hurtful things" a long list of human tribulations, ranging from quarrels and robberies to murders and war.[22] The explanation is for him an unbreakable one, going beyond any man-made remedy. Man's sin explains both the necessity of political constraints and the necessarily defective quality of all political institutions. With many states, he once wrote, we have wars among them; given a world state, we would have wars within it.[23] The thought finds its echo in the present when George Kennan defines the conduct of government as a "sorry chore ... devolving upon civilized society, most unfortunately, as a result of man's irrational nature, his selfishness, his obstinacy, his tendency to violence." [24] There is here an attractive world-weary wisdom as well as a valuable caution against expecting too much from changes in forms and in-

20. Clyde Kluckhohn, *Mirror for Man* (New York, 1949), p. 277.
21. W. Fred Cottrell, "Research to Establish the Conditions for Peace," *The Journal of Social Issues,* XI (1955), p. 20.
22. St. Augustine, *The City of God,* tr. Marcus Dods, Bk. XXII, ch. xxi.
23. *Ibid.,* Bk. XIX, ch. vii.
24. George F. Kennan, *Realities of American Foreign Policy* (Princeton, 1954), p. 48.

stitutions. Yet the first image, if rigidly held, becomes sterile. The search for causes is an attempt to account for differences. If men were always at war, or always at peace, the question of why war, or why peace, would never arise. What does account for the alternation of periods of war and peace? Human nature no doubt plays a role in bringing about war. Human nature, however, cannot by itself explain both war and peace, except by the simple statement that man's nature is such that sometimes he fights and sometimes he does not. And this statement leads inescapably to the attempt to explain why he fights sometimes and not others. The partial quality of the first image leads us to go beyond it in seeking the understanding that enables one to account for differences.

In a second image of international relations the basic causes of war are found in the political structures and social, economic conditions of the separate states. The initial argument is that all wars can be attributed to defects in some or in all states. The statement is then often reversed: If bad states make wars, good states would live at peace with one another. With varying degrees of justification this view has been attributed to Plato and Kant, to nineteenth-century liberals and revisionist socialists. Differing in their descriptions of good states as well as on the problem of bringing about their existence, they agree on the principle involved. Thus Thomas Hill Green, liberal-idealist of the mid-nineteenth century, saw no reason why states, as they improve internally, "should not arrive at a passionless impartiality in dealing with each other. . . ."[25] But how good would good states have to be before most occasions for conflict among them would disappear and those remaining could consistently be settled by cold reason? This question endures even if one can imagine a process by which the generalization of a single pattern of the state could take place.

In a third image, the locus of major causes is found neither in men nor in states but in the state system itself. The first and second images are criticized not so much as being wrong but as being incomplete. Their partial qualities drive one to seek the more inclusive nexus of causes. The old problem of political philosophy — do men create the societies and states in which they live or do those societies

25. Thomas Hill Green, *Lectures on the Principles of Political Obligation,* par. 175.

and states, so to speak, remake the men who live in them? — here appears in a different form. Rousseau has argued that the sources of conflict are not so much in men as they are in society. In asking if a man would not be a fool to enclose and cultivate a piece of land when the first comer may rob him of the fruits of all his toil, he puts his point negatively.[26] In commenting upon "the most perfect society imaginable" that would presumably exist among "a people of true Christians," he notes that "all the citizens without exception would have to be equally good Christians; if by ill hap there should be a single self-seeker or hypocrite . . . he would certainly get the better of his pious compatriots."[27] He thus implies a criticism that, with terms changed, applies to the second as well as the first image. One cannot begin to behave decently unless he has some assurance that others will not be able to ruin him. This thought Rousseau develops and applies to states existing in a condition of anarchy in his fragmentary essay on "The State of War" and in his commentaries on the works of the Abbé de Saint-Pierre. A state may want to behave peacefully; it may have to consider undertaking a preventive war, for the nations of Europe are willful units in close juxtaposition with rules neither clear nor enforceable to guide them. This is his basic explanation for the behavior of all of them, though with Alexander Hamilton he would add that to presume a lack of hostile motives among states is to forget that men are "ambitious, vindictive, and rapacious." A monarchical state may go to war because the vanity of its king leads him to seek glory in military victory; a republic may go to war because of the folly of its assembly or because of its commercial interests. That the king be vain, the assembly foolish, or the commercial interests irreconcilable: none of these is inevitable. However, so many and so varied are the causes of war among states that "to look for a continuation of harmony between a number of independent, unconnected sovereigns in the same neighborhood, would be to disregard the uniform course of human events, and to set at defiance the accumulated experience of the ages."[28] The third image while not excluding the

26. Jean Jacques Rousseau, *A Discourse on the Origin of Inequality* in *The Social Contract and Discourses*, tr. G. D. H. Cole (New York, 1950), p. 212.
27. *The Social Contract*, pp. 135-136. I have added to the English translation the word "equally" in order to render the French text more accurately.
28. *The Federalist Papers*, No. 6. Cf. No. 4 (Jay) and No. 7 (Hamilton).

first and second, places them in a defined perspective. This perspective is especially well developed in Rousseau, though one finds it in Hobbes, Hamilton and others as well.

Each image may be taken, optimistically, as a clue to necessary and sufficient prescriptions for peace or, more realistically, as a description of crucial difficulties under which men must live. The third image, moreover, makes clear why, in the absence of tremendous changes in the factors included in the first and second images, war will be perpetually associated with the existence of separate sovereign states.

There is, at least in the United States, a certain uneasiness among teachers and students of international relations. The uneasiness is rooted in a pervading ambivalence in the attitude toward one's subject matter. At one extreme, it is argued that international relations is a discipline as coherent and respectable as sociology, anthropology, or political science itself. This definition of the field is displayed in the curricula of some universities where international relations has achieved the status of a separate department. It is manifest as well in a number of books, notably in Quincy Wright's recent work, *The Study of International Relations,* in which the substance of international relations becomes a synthesis of all possibly relevant knowledge. At the other extreme it is sometimes argued that, far from being a discipline, international relations is not even a subject. It is instead a collection of diverse materials ordinarily within the province of historians, economists, geographers, social psychologists, and others, all related in some vaguely defined manner to the problems posed by relations among states. In the absence of a system for ordering its materials, the study of international relations is fairly placed in the second category. Such study may produce many insights, but they remain like a number of pearls, or glass beads, lying around loose. Their value may be great, but to separate the pearls from the beads a jeweller's glass is required, and, once the pearls have been selected, their use is slight unless they can either be placed in a setting or put on a string. One can, of course, order his materials on a common sense basis without a full-blown political theory. Such efforts, though impressive in some ways, often result either in sterile systems of classification that fail to interrelate seemingly disparate materials causally and dynamically, or they display erratic and naive judgment in the attempt to comprehend the movement of the real world. One may differ on how great these dangers are, but none would assert that they are absent.

The argument here advanced is not that the gathering of data can neither lend credence to nor cast doubt upon the abstractions that theorists construct, that empirical investigation is, compared with theorizing, an activity of lesser dignity and worth. The argument is instead that more frequent and more systematic concern by the student of international relations with the classics of political philosophy can help him to order and comprehend the data with which he must work and to improve his critical judgment of statements of cause and interrelation. The function of political philosophy is to help to form, sharpen, and critically ground the fundamental understandings that we all build up somehow in our minds. Partial theories then elaborate, complicate, and contribute immediate relevance. The first without the second can be sterile; the second without the first can easily produce either chaos or a pseudo-scientific scholasticism.

Chapter V

INTERNATIONAL POLITICAL THEORY FROM OUTSIDE

BY CHARLES P. KINDLEBERGER

I

THE ANSWER to every significant question in economics is "It depends." This feeble aphorism signifies that all we have in economics are partial theories. What they tell us about the real world depends upon the circumstances. What happens to purchases when price goes up? It depends. If expectations are inelastic, and the market believes that price will return again to the normal level, buying declines. If expectations are elastic, on the other hand, and people believe that prices will rise further, consumers rush out to buy up supplies before hoarders get them. More will be bought.

There is no single, comprehensive economic theory, all embracing, all encompassing. There are large branches of the subject — microeconomics, which deals with the behavior of markets and firms, and macro-, treating the level of national income and fluctuations in total activity. These are loosely related in various ways. But they are not organically and umbilically joined, despite the promotional literature of textbook publishers. Within each branch, moreover, there is room for assorted partial theories, dealing with single variables — money, fiscal policy, capital, the rate of interest. In some fields, e.g., wages, the discipline lacks even an agreed partial theory. And in still other areas, such as international adjustment, partial theories have been worked out for price, holding income constant, or income, holding prices constant, but the task of synthesis is only partly accomplished.

Like meteorology, economics deals with many variables — and there is considerable public pressure for forecasting. It is possible by the use of mathematical techniques to elaborate models with complex expressions. Most of these fall short of reality because of the necessity to adopt simplifying assumptions. Many are too difficult to handle, whether by literary economists, or for the mathematician who lacks access to a computer. A recent taxonomic study on the balance of payments, working with 22 variables and 17 parameters and offering 28,781,143,379 possible outcomes,[1] was vigorously attacked for its failure to narrow down the possibilities to a workable and relevant range.

Like other sciences, economics chooses its interests from the world about it. The center of attention was occupied in the 1920's by war debts and reparations — the transfer problem; in the 1930's by national income determination and employment; today it is occupied by the problem of growth in underdeveloped countries. There is no one theory of economic growth. This economist and that has emphasized this variable and that: Schumpeter, innovation; Harrod and Domar, capital accumulation; Rosenstein-Rodan, external economies; Arthur Lewis, balance, and so forth. Economic growth, like economics in general, lacks a synthesis which combines its differing emphases into a single general theory.

Somewhat diffidently, I suggest that this condition in economic theory should encourage its sister social science, politics. Like politics, economics holds broad theory and theorists in the highest esteem, above and beyond specialists, empiricists, institutionalists and intuitionists. This status is accorded them less because their work is complete, or potentially useful, than because, in the sociology of knowledge, abstraction ranks ahead of concreteness. But I suspect that political theory would make more progress if it were to go back to producing partial theories to fit varying assumptions, rather than pursue that will o' the wisp, the general theory. Great men will doubtless continue to propound general theories — Keynes called his last book *The General Theory of Employment, Interest and Money*. But it remains for the rest of us to recognize that these turn out to be useful

---

1. See J. E. Meade, *The Balance of Payments, Mathematical Supplement* (London, 1951), p. 33 note.

partial theories or special cases, which complement rather than compete with theories put forward by rival masters. It is sterile to argue which is the more general theory; fruitful to see what special assumptions distinguish one partial theory from another or how two partial theories may be combined.

II

As the official analogizer from a sister science, I now turn to a theoretical question which has interested economists and which has a bearing on the distinction, if any, between politics in general and international politics. This is the difference between international and domestic trade. The classic economists from Hume (if we may share him with political theory) to Marshall held that the difference turned on the mobility of factors. Inside a country, the price of a commodity was kept in line by shifts of factors of production; if labor earned more manufacturing cloth in the Midlands than in London, migration equalized the wage rate and the price of cloth. Between nations, however, factor movements were held impossible. Prices were equalized, if at all, by movements of goods. In international trade, that is, goods markets alone are joined, while domestic trade combines both goods and factor markets.

Modern economists no longer subscribe to this view. Capital and labor can move internationally, and in the latter half of the nineteenth century did so on an impressive scale. In some cases — British capital and Italian emigrants — mobility was greater between than within countries. Ohlin has suggested that international and interregional trade are alike in involving the necessity to overcome space, and differ from the subject matter of domestic economics which adopts the simplifying assumption that all activity occurs at a single point. Other writers have emphasized the existence of different monetary units, and the necessity to convert one currency into another; or different banking and fiscal institutions, which may result in asymmetrical responses between countries, or different commercial policies. One modern ultra-classicist, Graham, has denied that there is validity in the concept of a country's demand or supply of a given commodity; in his view trade is carried on between buying and selling firms in whatever country they happen to be located, so that it makes no sense to add up separately the demands and offers of firms on each side of a national frontier.

There is currently fairly general agreement, however, that the differences in factor mobility, taste, space, money, fiscal systems, and commercial policies are superficial and that the fundamental distinction lies in the political and social cohesion of the trading units. Internal trade is among "us." International trade is between "us" and "them," as Friedrich List said more than a century ago. Among ourselves, we are prepared to operate a common set of rules, based on a common set of values. I do not propose to examine what these values are, or whether they are based on history, geography, genealogy, philosophy, philology, aesthetics or ethics; evidently all of them play a role in forming the basis for a nation or for a sharing unit. "We" adhere to a single monetary, wage, fiscal, commercial policy which affects all individuals within our boundaries regardless of their location. Between us and them, our government's task is to take care of us, and theirs to take care of them, using whatever monetary, fiscal, commercial and other national policies may be necessary to do so. Where the basis of our policies is social cohesion or integration, moreover, capital and labor move more readily internally than between countries.

What makes a geographic unit cohesive for this purpose? At least two possibilities exist as limiting cases, with a range of intermediate combinations. The units may be cohesive because of a common sense of belonging and acting together. We may call this a politically and socially "integrated" area. Or one or more classes or regions, alone or in combination, may make decisions for the wider group with the passive acceptance of or through the exercise of force over the active opposition of other classes or regions. For want of a better term we may call this a politically "structured" country. The common denominator is the capacity to make decisions, whether in the general or the particular interest, or some combination of the two, depending upon the degree of democratic consent on the one hand, and tradition, power, force and so forth on the other.

In the nineteenth century, there was a measure of world integration which produced an approach to free trade and the gold standard. In some views, this was a regime imposed on the world by Britain, and can thus be regarded as a "structured" solution, rather than a product of world integration. But the bourgeois all over the world, to credit Marx with a grain of truth, shared a common set of values and a common culture. World integration excluded large segments of the earth in Asia, Africa and Latin America, except for enclaves. International integration for this class was accompanied by national non-integration as income distribution within countries was widely skewed, democracy limited, and the bulk of society parochial and regional. Even political unification in Germany and Italy brought little political, social or economic integration. Tariff protection in wheat and iron was imposed on Germany by the Junkers and Ruhr steel interests, and against the interests of the peasants, workers and steel fabricators.

The position changed after world war and depression. By 1939 attention was focused on national policy, which is made, explicitly at least, in the general interest of all classes rather than the particular interest of entrepreneurs. New tasks have been undertaken by government. The enlarged budget requires higher levels of taxation and presents an opportunity for greater income redistribution in favor of equality.

The distinction between a budget and a market is important. The former is a sharing mechanism, in which an attempt is made to equalize burdens. In setting a budget there may be a degree of shifting burdens from one group to another, and this can be carried so far, through tax evasion and corruption, that the national integrity is threatened, as in France today. A budget is also, like a market, a planning means for making choices among unlimited wants with scarce means. But when it operates successfully, the budget is, in an important respect, a device which reflects a common understanding of the need for sharing burdens. Families, towns, states, nations agree on common expenditures and allocate benefits and costs on sharing rather than market considerations. Samuelson has suggested that the pure theory of federal expenditure should deal with those items like national defense, roads, public parks, and street lighting which are indivisible in consumption: their enjoyment by one person does not reduce the amount available for others. But families share food and clothing, which is purchased with the earnings of one or two breadwinners, and local governments could sell housing, education, hospital care, at cost rather than make them available on the basis of need. The budget differs from the market as a Christian, loving his neighbor, differs from the economic man, who maximizes his personal profit.

This distinction between a budget and a market is significant for international trade theory today. International trade runs between sharing units which do not share between themselves. It is possible to think of the wants of a whole country, because a country, as a political and social unit committed to principles of sharing through budgetary process, will redistribute income automatically when changes in international prices bring about changes in the distribution of income within the society. Part of the equilibrating process in interregional trade which is not present in international trade involves net taxation on some regions and net subsidies to others. The taxes and subsidies are not, as a rule, designed to be regional in their incidence, but can be regarded in this light after aggregation of their effects on individuals and local communities. Economists who object to net taxation on, say, New England, in the interest of that region, are fundamentally objecting to the basis of the federal union which is attempting to achieve equity among individuals, wherever located. To focus on the regional effect is to divide the "us" into a smaller us and a residual them. When this occurs over a significant enough series of problems, the national unit is preserved only by force, as in Spain, or in geographic terms, but as an economic and political fiction.

Since 1939 this difference between international and interregional trade has again altered. Lend-lease in wartime, and the Marshall plan in postwar reconstruction, involve international sharing which contrasts with President Coolidge's "They hired the money, didn't they?" NATO has evolved some rudimentary practice in sharing defense expenditures. Point IV and UN Technical Assistance involve certain subsidies to underdeveloped countries.

In wartime, the capacity to share is heightened by the enhanced perception of the linkage of interests. Aid for relief, as in UNRRA or disaster loans and grants, is fairly readily forthcoming either because the donor fears the unrest and disruption which would occur if he failed to take steps, or because the need is so dramatically brought home to him that the donor can imagine himself in the same position, and has compassion for others as a form of indulgence to himself.

International sharing, however, is much more difficult than national, in the absence of common items of expenditure for mutual benefit.

The allocation of capital contributions to the International Bank and International Monetary Fund or the international distribution of operating expenses of the United Nations or the League of Nations involves a most difficult task. There are no principles on which sharing can take place, and no heritage of experience on which small marginal changes can be grafted from year to year. With benefits and costs unequally distributed, the process is more like charity — in its early unorganized stages — where sharing is voluntary rather than a duty under a broad surrender of political power to a community. The difference between charity and taxation is narrowing within communities as giving becomes more organized, but in the absence of substantial budgets for agreed purposes, it remains wide between political units.

You will forgive, I hope, this long excursus into what may be, to those of you who are not international-trade economists, not a very interesting problem. I am trying to suggest, however, contrary to what others in this series have held, that there is a difference in kind between national and international politics, as I think there is a difference between national and international economics. The nature of the difference is elusive, and changing. As the European Coal and Steel Community lives on in its sixth year, it is necessary to ask again whether sovereignty is really indivisible. The same question arises for customs unions and common markets. But it seems to me that international political theory concerns the relations between governmental units which, up to now for the most part, have been interested in maximizing the welfare of the state and its citizens. Domestic politics, on the other hand, today takes place within the framework of some sort of compact, under which the various elements in society have agreed to limit the pursuit of their interest beyond a certain point where it would begin to impinge on the interests of the other parties to the compact. Strains of self-interest on the part of groups within the state may disrupt the compact and lead as far as revolution. Or the state may be hierarchically structured with little consent employed to resolve conflicts of interest regularly and automatically through sharing arrangements.

Economists recognize that trade within a country which has large "non-competing groups" partakes of the nature of international rather than interregional trade. The classic case is the North and the South of the United States, where until after World War I labor did not move north despite the higher wages, nor capital south despite higher rates of interest. Where the class structure within a country becomes sharply separated, or regional interests dominate at the expense of the national, the theory of international politics should be applied to the constituent elements instead of the theory of domestic politics.

It may be argued that nations themselves are grouped into units for various purposes, whether NATO, the Organization of American States, the British Commonwealth of Nations, or even that most intangible of units which acts together for many purposes, Canada and the United States. Or it may be held that international law constitutes a compact limiting the actions of states and reducing their interrelations to the level of the domestic. Neither of these lines of reasoning persuades me. Where relations run between groupings of countries on the same level, — a Grand Alliance and a Triple Entente, or a NATO and a Sino-Soviet bloc — it may be appropriate to develop a special theory for those relations in which the international group is primary. But for most purposes, the nation is the primary group, not the international community. There may be elements of international politics in relations between component parts of a state, and elements of domestic politics in relations between states. By and large, however, international politics is the politics of separately maximizing units; domestic, the politics of parts of an integral whole.

III

Has economics anything more to offer by way of analogy? and in particular anything on the substance? As one who has tried to teach that governments are not like families in the necessity to live within their income to avoid bankruptcy, I am not unaware of the danger of analogies. The substance of politics is in many respects different from that of economics, and some of these differences will be indicated in what follows. Nonetheless let me continue this headlong rush into territory proscribed for angels, by suggesting that it is a mistake to look for a single variable which an integral political unit is trying to maximize in the same way in all circumstances. It is important to distinguish first of all the degree of power possessed by the state, and second, the length of time over which it is trying to maximize.

In economics, we can cope best with the situation where the individual firm has no power. Power in this sense is power over price. In pure competition a firm is small, and is one among numerous competitors. No feasible change in output by the firm will affect the price at which it sells. If I am allowed to summarize summarily, the position can be put like this:

	Firms Lack Power	*Power Unequally Divided Among Firms and Factors*	*Power Equally Divided Among Firms and Factors*
Short-Run Maximization	Pure competition	(monopoly or (monopsony (oligopolistic (competition	strikes price wars
Long-Run Maximization		(price leadership (dominant firm	stable prices (approaching long-run cost?) countervailing power

Using general characterizations rather than economic jargon, one can fill the boxes as follows:

short-run	} atomistic {	exploitive	antagonistic
long-run		paternalistic	cooperative

This schema by no means exhausts the possibilities. Given a monopolist seller and a monopoly buyer or monopsonist, both maximizing in the short run, one arrives at bilateral monopoly, for which we have no determinate solution. This is cold war. With two long-run monopolists one can arrive at different solutions depending upon the degree of sophistication each competitor imputes to the other. There will be one outcome if each acts independently, and another if each takes into account the probable conduct of his competitor. Or one can postulate the existence of numerous weak competitors in a field dominated by a monopolist, or fought over by two short-run competing monopolists. Do they proclaim neutrality, constitute a third force, or join forces with one (by merger or alliance) for fear of being gobbled up by the other? What happens when a short-run maximizer collides with a long-run maximizer, each with power? Will the long-run firm appease by yielding market to the aggressive firm? Where will it draw the line? Will the expanding firm become satisfied through increasing sales, turn inward on problems of production, or will appetite feed on victory? In these questions which have relevance to international politics, there is need for a theory of bargaining.

The analogy between a market and a balance-of-power situation raises an important question of the stability conditions. Pure competition cannot last with decreasing costs. Sooner or later some firm will end up producing the entire output of the industry, having absorbed or destroyed the other original firms. Similarly a country cannot long endure at an equilibrium level of national income if any change in income brings about a larger change in consumption and investment. A slight departure from the original equilibrium will be cumulative, and inflation will gain speed until it explodes in hyperinflation. What corresponds in the balance of power to the stability condition of increasing costs in pure competition or of a willingness to save some portion of any increase in income? It is perfectly clear that there are those who favor power politics because they think balance-of-power situations are for the most part stable, while others, who think that the balance of power always degenerates into war, regard it as unstable.

I am certainly unwilling to discuss on the basis of ignorance the stability conditions in the balance of power. One aspect of the question should be investigated in the relations between the power of the two groups. So long as power is evenly matched, stability may be high, whereas a marked outdistancing by one or the other may lead to explosion. Another consideration worthy of investigation is the reversibility of various steps in the building of an alliance, or at least the expectation of the possibility of change. So long as there is a remote possibility that any member of the alliance of some significant strength can be pried loose and induced to switch sides — an Italy before World War I, or Yugoslavia today—the balance may be stable.

But to return to bargaining. Schelling has observed that it is often a strength in bargaining to proclaim weakness. The car marked **AUTO SCHOOL** is given a wide berth. Of course, it also helps to be strong; the right of way is even more readily accorded to the 50-ton trailer truck. To pursue this new analogy a little further, let us grant that today's automobiles have power. We assume that the short-run interest is to get from one place to another in the shortest possible time, while the long-run interest includes survival of car and driver. The system is viable if all participants in the traffic game maximize their long-run interest without altogether neglecting their interest in getting where they are going, and leads to chaos if none do. But the game can be played if a few drive madly in pursuit of their short-run interests — say ambulances, fire engines, and police cars, with a private driver or two thrown in — provided they signal effectively what is taking place. These short-run maximizers are tolerable within limits; traffic will make way for them. In a market, sales territory will be yielded to the "chiselers," provided they indicate clearly that they are operating within limits and will not jeopardize the long-run interests of the others. Even where convention or law precludes communication it may be possible to restrain competition if each competitor unmistakably understands the intentions of the other. Warring armies in the field are prepared to limit the use of weapons, use restraint in the treatment of prisoners and civilians, etc., provided that these limitations are recognized on both sides.

Notice that in these analogies power and self-interest are distinct. What is power? In his essay on economic sovereignty, the economist Hawtrey has defined it as the capacity to produce and transport goods. With the British navy in mind, he had regard particularly to the capacity to deliver firepower at a distance. But this is too narrow. In a market, in a traffic situation, and I suspect in international politics, power is the capacity to affect others without being as much affected. Where dominance occurs, the relationship is completely asymmetrical. But where force is balanced, power vanishes in a stalemate. Power includes a large element of prestige. When everybody is somebody, nobody is anybody. Force is additive; more for one participant does not change the amount for the other. Power, on the other hand, is even more mysterious than the pie of constant diameter in which one consumer can gain only at the expense of the other. When the pie is evenly divided it disappears. But a small change can make it reappear again, bigger and better than ever.

It is thus misleading, in my view, to regard politics as the production and distribution of power in simple analogy to income in economics. Power in both economics and politics is an aid to maximization, but not its object. Profit is clearly the object of short-run maximization in economics. But in the long run, this will not do. Profits are not neglected when time is considered. But corporations frequently neglect to raise prices to the market-equilibrium level — *vide* the automobile position in 1946-48. A long-run maximizing oligopolist is likely to be uncomfortable when a substantial competitor goes bankrupt; thereafter responsibility toward the public, toward labor and toward government lies more squarely on his shoulders. Profitable opportunities will be shunned if they run the risk of damaging a reputation with one group interest or another. Contributions to charity, to public causes, and wage scales above the marginal product of workers attest to long- rather than short-run considerations. Some economists have argued that the only variable that the oligopolist can unambiguously be said to maximize is his survival.

In the long run, the national interest is also the preservation of the community. The short-run national interest is more difficult to identify. Frequently the means are confused with the end, and power becomes an end in itself. National prestige, territory, a particular irredenta, trade opportunities, colonies, satellites occasionally become paramount goals. Or the short-run interest may coincide with the long and be the right to be left alone.

It is difficult to build a useful model of social behavior when the object to be maximized is imprecise, may differ from one actor to another, or when the two objectives of the two actors are clearly incompatible. Economics has the great benefit of a clear-cut short-run objective — profits. In the long run, when the object of the firm is merely to survive, the prediction of behavior takes on greater difficulty. In international politics, the long-run goal may be said to be no more precise than in economics and in the short run it is clearly less so.

In internal politics, under democratic conditions, there is at least agreement on a long-run goal. Political forces may struggle over the distribution of power, but there is an implicit agreement that power will not be used to destroy the loser in the battle. Where this agreement is lacking, as in Spain or South Africa or between German and Jew in 1939, the country may survive as a geographical expression, but undergo fundamental social metamorphosis.

In economics some settlement of duopoly or short-run maximizing oligopoly is likely to be found, since the object of the game, mere money, is divisible. Competitors may concert and try to milk consumers or suppliers, or they find some basis for compromise in sharing profits. In domestic politics, moreover, many struggles are over income, and the contestants are usually agreed that the struggle will stop short of the destruction of one of them. In international politics, this is not necessarily the case. The short-run objectives of Egypt and Western Europe, of Israel and the Arab Nations, of India and Pakistan in Kashmir may be mutually contradictory. No form of words will reconcile the irreconcilable, and agreements like Yalta and Potsdam, or decision to turn the matter over to the United Nations, raise hopes which are doomed to disappointment. Solution between an Israel determined to survive and Arab states which regard Israel as a threat to their own survival cannot be negotiated by lawyers, no matter how clever at finding compromise among conflicting elements of a political unit. The only solution is to temporize to prevent open conflict and allow time for attitudes to change on one side or both. In this process, be it noted, the power balance, and with it the volume of power, may undergo drastic alteration.

When does a firm have regard to its long-run interest instead of its short? When is it interested in maintaining its competitors, in treating its employees generously, in holding down prices, (in a trade union, wages), in the public interest, and casting bread on the waters in subsidies to schools, hospitals and other public benefits where the return is indirect if not intangible? When does a country act in its narrow interest or have regard for the broader international community?

The cynical answer is that the poor and lean compete, the rich and fat turn to the long-run interest, in which they propose to survive at something like the same or an expanded level of living. Dealings between the haves and the have-nots are thus inevitably fraught with misunderstanding and friction such as arises in this country's relations with India, Egypt, Guatemala. Only where the poor decide that they advance their short-run interests fastest by lining up with the long-run goals of the rich will there be apparent harmony. Between the extremes of lean and fat, the aggressive competitor, the chiseler, the disrupter of power balance and the aggressor pushing out into power vacua is the johnny-come-lately who has acquired power but is still maximizing in the short run. If his concern shifts quickly to the long-run, there is not likely to be difficulty. If on the other hand, he pushes forward successfully and continuously without meeting opposition, he will understand that previous holders of power are prepared to let it slip, and even to lose their own long-run interest in survival. Accordingly it is important to signal that reckless driving will not be condoned, and that a reckless foreign policy of aggression will be condemned.

Is there anything of a more positive nature to be done? It runs counter to the narrow short-run interest of the United States to build up the strength and prosperity of Western Europe and to accelerate the economic development of underdeveloped countries, now too poor to take the appropriate economic steps in their own long-run interest. In the short run, these measures cost money and dissipate the power of this country. But over a period of time it is desirable that third, fourth and fifth forces come into being: the Aluminum Company of America can rejoice in the success of Reynolds and Kaiser, although anti-trust laws may prevent it from extending development loans and granting technical assistance. The day may come when the Soviet Union and the United States are able to give more attention to their long-run interest in survival as members of the world community and less to the short-run expansive designs of the former and containment policies of the latter. The United States cannot shift to the long-run basis of maximization by itself. But if the Soviet Union were to extend its horizon, and the United States to follow, another opportunity would be afforded for a demonstration that when economic and political man maximizes in the long run, rather than the short, it is impossible to distinguish him from the Christian.

Chapter VI

The Actors in International Politics

BY ARNOLD WOLFERS

IN THEORIZING about almost any feature of international politics, one soon becomes entangled in a web of controversy. Even the identity of the "actors" — those who can properly be said to perform on the international stage — is a matter of dispute which raises not unimportant problems for the analyst, for the practitioner of foreign policy, and for the public. If the nation-states are seen as the sole actors, moving or moved like a set of chess figures in a highly abstract game, one may lose sight of the human beings for whom and by whom the game is supposed to be played. If, on the other hand, one sees only the mass of individual human beings of which mankind is composed, the power game of states tends to appear as an inhuman interference with the lives of ordinary people. Or, take the diplomat who sees himself as accredited to an entity called Indonesia or France: he may behave quite differently from the diplomat who considers his mission addressed to specific individuals or to ruling groups or to a people. A statesman accustomed to an analysis of international politics in terms of state behavior alone will treat the United Nations differently from one who believes in the rise of international organizations to a place of independent control over world events similar to that exerted by states.

Until quite recently, the "states-as-the-sole-actors" approach to international politics was so firmly entrenched that it may be called the traditional approach. After the Napoleonic wars, nation-states, particularly the European "Great Powers," as they were called, replaced the image of the princes or kings of former centuries as the sovereign, independent, single-minded actors, the movers of world events. To "nation-states" were ascribed the acts that accounted for changes in the distribution of power, for alignments and counter-alignments, for expansion and colonial conquest, for war and peace — the chief events in international affairs whenever a multitude of sovereigns have been in contact with one another. The concept of a multi-state system composed of entities of strikingly similar character and behavior appeared realistic to observers and analysts.

Starting in the period between the two world wars and gaining momentum after World War II, a reaction set in against the traditional states-as-actors approach. This reaction has taken two distinct forms: one new theory has placed individual human beings in the center of the scene that had previously been reserved to the nation-states; the other emphasized the existence, side by side with the state, of other corporate actors, especially international organizations. Both reactions have led to valuable new insights and deeper understanding of the dynamics of world politics, but they are in fact supplements to the traditional theory rather than substitutes for it.

I

The "individuals-as-actors" approach first appeared in the form of what has been called the "minds-of-men" theory of international politics. It was soon to be followed by the "decision-making" approach which was a reaction against tradition from another angle. Both demanded that attention be focused on individual human beings as actors. Together, the new schools of thought represent a swing of the pendulum from an extreme "state" emphasis to an equally extreme emphasis on the men who act for states. Both must be credited with a humanization of international politics, as it has been called, by attracting attention to the human element which had been minimized in the traditional approach. It was the aim of the new theories to replace the abstract notion of the state with the living realities of human minds, wills, and hearts. But the result, on the whole, was to substitute one set of abstractions for another, because, in politics, it is also an abstraction to examine the individual apart from the corporate bodies by means of which he acts politically.

The minds-of-men approach received its emotional stimulus from two sources: the realization that, in the age of mass communication, propaganda, and ideological movements, there were growing opportunities for the masses to play a significant role in international affairs, and a general desire to see the masses take advantage of these opportunities. To stress men rather than states and thus to focus attention on the common man — traditionally more the victim than the beneficiary of international politics — seemed to offer a way out of conflict, war, and power politics generally. It is not surprising that UNESCO should have become an exponent of the theory, since it was established, as Dunn points out,[1] with a view to constructing peace in the minds of men. The Utopian undertones of many early pronouncements by those who espoused the new approach were unmistakable, but should not deflect from the contribution which the new approach can make to the realistic understanding of world affairs.

Most of the criticism of the states-as-actors theory implicit in the new approach turns on the distinction between genuine human needs and what appear to be the a-human interests of the state. There are those who claim that too great an emphasis on the role of states and their interests in power, prestige, territory, and the like, will divert political action from the satisfaction of the common man's real needs and desires to the service of the few who can parade their interests as those of the nation. Is it credible, they ask, that Egyptian fellaheen and Pakistani peasants, desperately in need of food, shelter, and improved conditions of health, should, as their governments contend, yearn for the satisfaction of such "state interests" as the liquidation of Israel or the unification of Kashmir under Pakistani rule, when the pursuit of such interests requires great sacrifices of the masses? Does the state not take on the character of an a-human monster to whom dignity is given gratuitously, if it is regarded as an actor in its own right, at liberty to place its interests above those of the human beings that compose it?

However, one may question whether the quest for national security and power, for national independence, aggrandizement, or unification is any less "human" — and therefore necessarily less appealing to the masses — than the quest for food, shelter, comfort, and happiness. Actually, the minds-of-men theory and its humanization

1. Frederick S. Dunn, *War and the Minds of Men* (New York, 1950), pp. xi-xiv.

of international politics must be carried several steps farther than its exponents have done. Any analysis of the dynamics of international politics must take into account the fact that man is more than a private individual concerned only with his personal welfare or with the welfare of his family. Often enough he is ready to compromise his own well-being for the benefit of the groups and organizations with which he identifies himself. Psychologically, nothing is more striking today than the way in which men in almost every part of the globe have come to value those possessions upon which independent national statehood depends, with the result that men, in their public capacity as citizens of a state, are willing to make the most sweeping sacrifices of their own well-being as private individuals in the interest of their nation. Therefore, "state interests" are indeed human interests — in fact, the chief source of political motivation today.

One can argue that a nationalistic age has distorted men's pattern of values or that the manipulators of public opinion are chiefly responsible for this distortion. Nevertheless, the fact remains that a sufficient number of men identify themselves with their state or nation to justify and render possible governmental action in the name of "state interests." To say that something is in the interest of the state is like saying that a good roof is in the interest of the house, when what one really means is that a good roof is considered vital by the house's inhabitants who value the safety, completeness, and reputation of their residence.

There is, however, nothing absolute or unchanging about the value men attach to state interests. The position of the value of national unification, for instance, in the hierarchy of values, especially its position relative to particular private needs and desires, is subject to change and differs from group to group and from individual to individual. Therefore, it is proper to be aware of individuals as the actors behind the scene, so to speak, whenever needs and interests, private or public, come into play in international affairs. Whether a state has a "vital interest" — in access to the sea or in the return of a lost province, for example — depends on the relative values attached by its citizens to these national objectives, on the one hand, and to private interests which would be sacrificed in the pursuit of the national objectives, on the other. In losing sight of the individuals who comprise a state, exponents of the states-as-actors theory may come up with a relatively accurate analysis of national behavior in a period when value patterns remain static, but they are more likely to be mistaken in a period of upheaval in which elites and values are subjected to rapid and radical change. One wonders today, for instance, whether the bulk of the population in countries facing the risks of nuclear war will long continue to regard as vital, and thus worthy of defense in war, all the "state interests" that they were once ready to place in this category. Other signs point to the likelihood that the masses, who have gained greater influence as behind-the-scenes actors, will push for greater restraints upon the pursuit of those state interests — such as national security or prestige — that are seen to conflict with private welfare needs. Such a development will not indicate that individuals are suddenly taking over the function formerly performed by states, but rather that larger bodies of individuals are sharing the role once reserved to the members of small elites who formerly decided what the "national interest" demanded or justified. It would always have been possible to interpret international politics through an examination of the individuals who were responsible for state action — the "humanizing" approach. But it must be recognized that in the course of the present century the number of these individuals has been greatly enlarged.

The failure to see man in his double capacity, as a private individual and as a political being, accounts for an illusion common among the more idealistic exponents of the minds-of-men approach. Although they assume that better understanding between peoples opens the safest path to peace, Dunn has pointed out that peoples who know and understand each other perfectly may nevertheless become involved in war.[2] The explanation for this apparent paradox is not hard to find, provided one thinks in terms of the whole man rather than solely in terms of his private aims and desires. If one were in contact with the people of the Soviet Union today, one would probably find them preoccupied with the tasks of furthering their personal welfare, happiness, and social advancement in much the same way as any similar group of men in the United States. The discovery of such similarities of interest and aspiration tends to arouse a sense of

2. *Ibid.,* p. 7.

sympathetic understanding; it certainly does not provoke fear or serve to justify policies based on the expectation of international conflict. As a result, people who think exclusively in terms of private individuals and who experience harmonious relationships with citizens of "hostile" countries are inclined to see nothing but unhappy misunderstanding, if not evil, in the way governments act toward one another. Yet, the fact that Americans and Russians, in much the same fashion, pursue the same goals when acting as private individuals gives no indication of their aims as citizens who are concerned with national interests of their respective countries. Here, there is far less chance that their aims will be found to be in harmony. In fact, better understanding may merely reveal the incompatibility of their respective objectives. Thus, it may be revealed that Russians, if good Marxists, want their government to drive Capitalism toward its inescapable doom, or, if good nationalists, to secure safe access to warm water ports. At the same time, Russians may find that their American counterparts demand the containment, if not elimination, of Communist tyranny, and a halt to Russian expansion before it reaches the Mediterranean or Persian Gulf and endangers American security. It appears, then, that to humanize the image of world politics by penetrating to the minds and hearts of living actors does not necessarily give us a more peaceful picture of the world. As long as men identify themselves with their nation and cling to such national possessions as sovereign independence, territorial integrity, and national security, the establishment of harmonious private relations across national borders will have little impact on the course of international political events and encounters.

It is therefore clear that an exclusive minds-of-men approach with its concentration on the motives and activities of individual actors is inadequate and misleading. It is undeniable that men alone, and not states, are capable of desires and intentions, preferences and feelings of friendship or hatred; men, not states, can be tempted or provoked, can overestimate or underestimate their own country's power relative to the power of other states, and can establish the goals of national policy and sacrifices consistent with national security. However, although nothing can happen in the world arena unless something happens inside of scores of men's minds and hearts, psychological events are not the whole stuff out of which international politics is formed. If they were, the political scientist would have to leave the field to the psychologist. The minds-of-men approach, while able to render important and indispensable services to a comprehensive theory of international politics, cannot do justice to all the essential events that fill the international arena. There can be no state behavior except as the term is used to describe the combined behavior of individual human beings organized into a state. Not only do men act differently when engaged in pursuing what they consider the goals of their "national selves," but they are able to act as they do only because of the power and influence generated by their nations as organized corporate bodies. Therefore, only when attention is focused on states rather than on individuals, can light be thrown on the goals pursued and means employed in the name of nations and on the relationships of conflict or cooperation, of power competition or alignment that characterize international politics. To abstract from these aspects of reality is as "unrealistic" as it is to abstract from the events occurring in the minds and hearts of the men who act in the name of the state. But because theory cannot proceed except by means of abstraction, it becomes necessary here to supplement one set of abstractions by the other and thus to remain cognizant of the double aspect of events that must be conceived as emanating simultaneously from individuals and from corporate bodies.

Thus a comprehensive theory does not call for a division of international politics into two compartments, one comprising the realm of the state as the actor in power politics, the other the realm of the human actors — the masses of common men with their psychological traits and their pursuit of human purposes. Instead, all the events occurring in the international arena must be conceived and understood from two angles simultaneously: one calling for concentration on the behavior of states as organized bodies of men, the other calling for concentration on human beings upon whose psychological reactions the behavior credited to states ultimately rests. One need only look closely at a feature as significant in high politics and as strongly stressed in the "states-as-actors" approach as the balancing of power process. Often it has been assumed that a process involving state power and its distribution among nations has a place in the states-as-actors approach alone and can be adequately treated by means of this approach. However, if one wishes to answer the question, for instance, whether the United States is in a position today to deter the Soviet Union by balancing the Soviet power, one cannot escape an examination of the psychology of individuals — in this case, of the leaders in the Kremlin. Deterrence can only work in the minds of the men in charge of Soviet policy by convincing them that acts they might otherwise wish to undertake would prove too costly in the light of the punishment the United States would, in their opinion, be able and prepared to inflict. It would be foolish, however, to go to the other extreme and try to comprehend the struggle for power between the two countries in purely psychological terms. The Soviet estimate of American resistance to acts of the USSR cannot be understood or predicted except as the objective facts concerning the respective power of the two states are taken into account. Moreover, the whole balancing process between the two antagonists, with its tremendous impact on world events, would drop from sight if attention were devoted exclusively to individuals or groups of individuals and to their psychological reactions.

As mentioned earlier, there has been a second reaction to the once firmly established states-as-actors theory that also implies a shift of attention to individuals and groups of individuals as the true actors. It has taken the form of what is properly called the "decision-making" approach, since it is concerned with decisions, with the way they are made, and with the men who make them. What interests us here is the role that this approach assigns to identifiable human beings and their predispositions. Although the emphasis on the decision-makers, like the emphasis on the minds of men, developed in protest against the states-as-actors theory, it was not also a reaction born of humanitarian or social considerations; it was provoked, instead, by the sweeping, seemingly over-simplified psychological and anthropological presuppositions on which the traditional theory rests.

If nation-states are conceived as the sole actors, it is inevitable that they be treated as if endowed, like human beings, with wills and minds of their own that permit them to reach decisions and to carry them out. Moreover, if state behavior is to be intelligible and to any degree predictable, states must be assumed to possess psychological traits of the kind known to the observer through introspection and through acquaintance with other human beings. States must be thought capable, for example, of desires and preferences, of satisfaction and dissatisfaction, of the choice of goals and means.

Actually, the states-as-actors theory postulates a limited number of such traits which, moreover, all states are assumed to have in common. States are presumed to possess a will to survive and a will to power; they live in fear of losing their possessions to others and are tempted by opportunities of acquiring new possessions. Because these basic traits are shared by *all* states, the exponents of the traditional approach can afford to treat these psychological presuppositions in a cavalier fashion. Little attention need be given to traits that, because they are constants or invariants, are incapable of helping to explain any differences in state behavior.

If all states were equally and constantly driven by fear, as Hobbes assumed — fear that their survival, the most cherished of their state possessions, might be threatened — the multi-state system would of necessity become an all-round struggle for security. If, instead, all states worthy of the name were as eager for expansion as Kjellén maintained, the ensuing struggle would turn on efforts at territorial acquisition and on counter-efforts at territorial preservation.

The decision-making approach questions the possibility of reaching realistic conclusions from any such crude and generally applicable psychological presuppositions. Its exponents insist that decisions and actions taken in the name of the state cannot be understood unless one penetrates to the individuals from whom they emanate. In contrast to what is implicit in the views of the opposing school, the basic hypothesis here is that all acts of states, as we are used to calling them, are vitally affected or determined by the particular predispositions of particular decision-makers or of particular groups of participants in the decision-making process. Thus, differences in such individual psychological traits as motivation, value preferences, temperament, and rationality are considered essential variables, and so are differences arising from affiliation of individuals with particular parties, agencies within the state, or with peoples of different culture.

One can illustrate the contrast between the two hypotheses by means of important past decisions in international politics. According to the states-as-actors theory, the American employment of the A-bomb over Hiroshima, or the American intervention in the war in Korea, could have been foreseen — to the extent to which foresight is possible at all — on the basis of the supposed common psychological disposition of states, coupled with an analysis of the existing circumstances which were external to the actors. Those who hold to the decision-making approach, on the contrary, consider it necessary to probe into the personal events that took place within the psyches of men like Stimson, Truman, and Acheson — and perhaps also of their advisors, backers, and opponents — and led them to choose one particular course of action rather than some alternative course.[3]

The decision-making approach naturally appeals to the historian who is interested in identifying the unique aspects of past events, which necessitates consideration of all conceivable variables, including the personal traits of particular human actors. But it poses a serious problem for the theorist whose task is not to establish the uniqueness of events but rather to gain a generalized knowledge of behavior in international politics, which means knowledge on a relatively high level of abstraction. Should he not, therefore, abstract from the personal predispositions of those who are instrumental in the making of decisions? If his use of the deductive method, as described earlier, permits him to formulate expectations of probable state behavior that prove relatively accurate, why should he take a time- and effort-consuming "detour" of the kind required by the decision-making approach and probe into the motivations of a Stimson or a Truman by an extensive empirical investigation? Could it be that the use of the A-bomb against Japan was predictable on the ground that "states tend to use their most powerful weapons," or American intervention in Korea by the proposition that "no great power, if it can help it, will permit its chief opponent to change the distribution of power by the unilateral use of military force?"

At first glance, it would seem as if the actual performance of a particular state could conform only by sheer coincidence with expec-

3. See Richard C. Snyder and Glenn D. Paige, "The United States' Decision to Resist Aggression in Korea: The Application of an Analytical Scheme," *Administrative Science Quarterly*, Vol. 3, No. 3, December 1958, especially pp. 348 and 374.

tations based on extremely crude generalizations about the way "states" tend to act under given circumstances. Why should the particular individuals responsible for United States policy in 1945 or 1950, men differing from others by a multitude of psychological features — motivations, idiosyncrasies, preferences, temperament — reach decisions of the kind the states-as-actors theory deduces from its abstract model? Yet a correlation in many instances between the predictions of theory and actual behavior is not accidental. It may be expected if two assumptions on which the theory rests are justified by the circumstances prevailing in the real world.

There is, first, the assumption mentioned above, that all men acting for states share the same universal traits of human nature. Specifically, these men are expected to place exceedingly high value on the so-called core possessions of the nation — above all, on national survival, national independence, and territorial integrity — and to react in fear against any threats to these possessions. It is also assumed that they share a strong inclination to profit from opportunities for the acquisition or re-acquisition of cherished national possessions, with national power as the chief means of preserving or acquiring national values. To the extent to which these traits are shared and have a decisive effect on the actions or reactions of statesmen and peoples, they create conformity as if by a kind of inner compulsion.

The second assumption concerns the environment in which governments are required to act. If it is true that the anarchical multistate system creates a condition of constant danger to national core possessions — specifically, to national survival — and, at the same time, provides frequent opportunity for new acquisitions, the actors can be said to act under external compulsion rather than in accordance with their preferences.

It is easy to see that both these sweeping assumptions are not the products of unrealistic fantasies. Attachment to possessions, fear, and ambition — though they vary in degree from man to man and from people to people — can properly be called "general traits of human nature," which are likely to operate with particular strength in men who hold positions of authority and national responsibility. That the condition of multiple sovereignty is one in which states "live dangerously" is also a matter of common experience and knowledge. The real question is whether internal and external pressures are strong enough everywhere and at all times to transform the actors into something like automatons lacking all freedom of choice. Certainly, to the degree that these compulsions exist in the real world, the psychological peculiarities of the actors are deprived of the opportunity to express themselves and can therefore be discounted as irrelevant to an analysis of international politics.

From illustrations of the effects of compulsion in private life, one can draw some conclusions as to the value of the two methods of approach.

Imagine a number of individuals, who vary widely in their predispositions, finding themselves inside of a house on fire. It would be perfectly realistic to expect that these individuals, with rare exceptions, would feel compelled to run for the exits. General fear of losing the cherished possession of life, coupled with the stark external threat to life, would produce the same reaction, whatever the psychological peculiarities of the actors. Surely, therefore, for an explanation of the rush for the exits, there is no need for an analysis of the individual decisions that produced it. The situation would be different if one or several members of the group had not joined the stampede, but had remained unmoved after the fire was discovered, or had even failed to perceive it. Such "deviationist" behavior, running counter to expectation, would justify and require intensive psychological inquiry.

A different situation would arise if, instead of being on fire, the house in question were merely overheated. In such a case, the second prerequisite of compulsion — serious external danger — would be absent. The reactions of different inhabitants might range all the way from hurried window-opening and loud complaints to complete indifference. Therefore, if one wished to formulate expectations concerning behavior in an overheated house, one would need intimate knowledge of varying individual predispositions and of the symptoms by which they could be recognized. Here, then, a decision-making approach would become necessary to supplement vague generalizations about reactions to discomfort that might be deduced from human nature in general, and such supplementation would become the more necessary the less overheated the house.

A second illustration should serve to show what is meant by compulsive action arising, not from external danger, but from an opportunity for gain. Here, the corresponding internal pressure for action comes from appetite or temptation rather than from fear. Let us assume that several individuals were attending a horse race, where they found themselves unable to see the race because of the crowds that had arrived before them. Suddenly an opening occurred in the ranks in front of them that offered an opportunity to move up close to the track. Under these circumstances, it would be reasonable to expect and predict that a rush to fill the gap would ensue. Here again, behavior could be explained or predicted, even with no knowledge about the individuals in question, by reference to a general trait of human nature — the desire for benefit or enjoyment — coupled with an external circumstance — the opening in the ranks. Here, also, a decision-making analysis would be useful only in regard to individuals who decided to remain where they were rather than to join the general and expected rush.

Much of what happens in international politics shows a striking resemblance with what has been described in the two cases from ordinary life. To take the case of the house on fire, it is easy to envisage an international situation in which both the external and internal factors — a dire and unmistakable threat to national survival, plus the fear it engendered among those responsible for state action — would place statesmen under the influence of almost irresistible compulsion. Instead of running for the exits, they would rush to enhance or maximize national power. When, for example, Mr. Acheson was advised not to favor the production of the first thermonuclear bomb, he is reported to have declared that its production was a matter of necessity and not of choice: in other words, that he was experiencing "compulsion," as the term is used here.

Appropriate examples can also be found to illustrate situations in the international arena that correspond to the race track metaphor. The most obvious example would be the powerful nation that finds itself bordering on a power vacuum. Since nations, like nature, are said to abhor a vacuum, one could predict that the powerful nation would feel compelled to fill the vacuum with its own power.

Yet, if one considers the conditions of danger and opportunity, of fear and appetite that have to exist in order to produce anything approaching inexorable compulsion, one will see that the highly abstract model used by the exponents of the states-as-actors theory cannot offer more than a first approximation to reality. Certainly, the employment of the states-as-actors theory in predicting the outcome of a crisis in which less than extreme compulsions were operative would prove dangerously unreliable and would need to be strictly qualified.

In international politics, the house is not always, nor everywhere, on fire although the temperature may not be comfortable, even under the best of circumstances! This means that danger as well as opportunity for gain and fear as well as appetite are not constants but important variables. The external threat to any South American republic today is incomparably less than the threats with which Israel or Iran have to cope. Nations, too, do not at all times stand in danger of losing the same values. It may be a threat to national independence in one instance, while merely the loss of an increment of security or of economic advantage in another.

Where less than national survival is at stake, there is far less compulsion and therefore a less uniform reaction. It is hard to predict the course that Nehru will follow as a consequence of the rather remote threats of the Cold War to India. On the other hand, any serious threat to India's control of eastern Kashmir can be expected to result in Indian military action, despite Nehru's alleged pacifist inclinations.

The differences in behavior arising from variations in the internal pressures are no less great. While a propensity for fear and an appetite for gain may be universal, men's reactions to danger and opportunity are far from identical and vary even among those who are responsible for the fate of their nation. Complacency no less than hysteria, and willingness to demand sacrifices no less than desire for popularity, affect the interpretation men give to what the "necessity of state" requires. Moreover, the "exits" are not clearly marked, with the result that some statesmen seek safety in military preparedness while others expect to find it in appeasement. Although statesmen who are entirely indifferent or blind to serious national danger and opportunity are the exception that proves the rule, it is hard to conceive of situations that leave no room at all for choice and thus for the expression of differences in psychology. While Eden believed Nasser's nationalization of the Suez Canal Company endangered Britain's economic lifeline and required military action, most other British statesmen would have reacted differently, and no one could have said with certainty at the time what course of action would have been the most rational under the circumstances. If Nasser had attacked the British homeland, thereby really "setting the house on fire," the reaction of any British government, whatever the personal traits of its members, could have been predicted.

From what has been said, it seems proper to conclude that the closer nations are drawn to the pole of complete compulsion, the more they can be expected to conform in their behavior and to act in a way that corresponds to the deductions that can be made from the states-as-actors model.

It is worth noting that a similar degree of conformity may be found where danger and compulsion are at a minimum. When not more than minor values are threatened by international discord, governments usually find it expedient to act according to established rules, since their interest in seeing others do likewise exceeds their interest in winning an occasional and minor advantage. Under these circumstances, they may forfeit an immediate national gain for the sake of sustaining the rule of law and its long-run benefits.

In war, compulsiveness and conformity are usually at a maximum, with the result that all nations feel compelled, for example, to employ the most effective weapons at their disposal. Hiroshima, as we said earlier, requires little if any decision-making analysis to explain the American action. Such an analysis might prove useful as a means of throwing light on varying attitudes of men or groups within the American government, some of whom opposed the use of the bomb on the grounds that victory was already assured and that there existed, therefore, no external compulsion requiring the application of the strongest weapon.

The American failure in the Korean War to use atomic bombs against tempting military targets north of the Yalu River is a far more promising area of decision-making analysis, because it represents a deviation from the practices one generally associates with warfare. The explanation may lie in a particularly high degree of foresightedness, or, as others believe, in an unusual degree of compliance with the wishes of friends and allies. In any case, General MacArthur, whose inclinations differed from those of the men charged with the final decision, might well have felt "compelled" to pursue the opposite course.

While there may be leeway for choice, and thus for the impact of psychological factors which distinguish individuals rather than abstract "states," it is by no means useless or misleading to take the relatively simple and very abstract states-as-actors model as an initial working hypothesis. Thus, in formulating expectations, it is possible and helpful to assume that no state will voluntarily make unilateral concessions to an opponent if these would seriously affect the existing distribution of power. When an exception to this general proposition is encountered, it calls for special analysis: for example, as a "deviationist" move, France's initiation of discussions on the Saar in 1949, pointing toward French withdrawal before West Germany itself had raised any such demand. Various explanations are possible — that France's fear of Germany was exceptionally strong or that French statesmen were exhibiting a unique degree of foresight in realizing that the French position would in time become untenable. The entry of the United States into the war in Korea represents another case of deviation, here from the usual disinclination of nations to take up arms unless "compelled" by an attack on vital national interests which, prior to the attack, South Korea was not considered to represent.

These illustrations indicate the particular services that the two theories on the "actors" are able to render. By establishing the "normal" actions and reactions of states in various international situations, the states-as-actors model sets a standard on which to base our expectations of state behavior and deviations. At the same time, a far more complex model is required if our expectations are to become sufficiently refined and realistic to take at least the predispositions of typical categories of decision-makers into account. There is no reason why intensive and comparative study of actual decisions should not, in time, provide much needed insight into the peculiarities in the behavior of such types of countries as those with dictatorial or democratic governments, with Asian or Western, Bolshevik or bourgeois elites, with predominantly military or civilian regimes, with a fanatical or a complacent public.[4] While it may be impractical to aim at knowledge about the decision-making of individual actors — if only because it is hard to foresee who will be the future decision-makers — it may prove useful to analyze the approach and behavior of certain "subnational" actors such as the business community, the trade union leaders, the Christian Democrats, or the American political parties. Only if it becomes possible to understand and predict typical kinds of nonconformist behavior can theory hope to approach reality. Moreover, because different degrees of compulsion will be operating at different times, it is not enough to know how states tend to act in situations of extreme danger or extreme temptation; one must also know what action to expect when the actors are relatively free to choose among alternative courses.

One example will serve to show what insight may be gained by applying the states-as-actors and the individuals-as-actors approaches simultaneously. Almost all analysts of international politics distinguish between nations that are satisfied with the *status quo* and others that are eager to change it. The controversial question is whether states fall into one category or the other primarily because of differences in the psychology of their leaders and peoples or because of differences in the objective conditions in which they find themselves. According to the states-as-actors theory which ignores the factor of possible psychological differences, objective or environmental factors alone can account for either a *status quo* or a revisionist attitude and behavior. This theory expects a nation to be revisionist if denied the enjoyment of any of its national core values, provided it has, or hopes to obtain, enough power to enable it to seek satisfaction of its objectives. Instead, an analyst who focuses on individual actors and their varying predispositions will look for an explanation of revisionist behavior primarily in such traits of statesmen as their peculiar aggressive and acquisitive appetites, their rebellious temperaments, or their subjective dissatisfactions.

In my opinion, empirical study would validate the hypothesis of the states-as-actors theory that almost any nation which has suffered a loss of territory or has been subjected to discrimination will, when

4. Morton A. Kaplan, *System and Process in International Politics* (John Wiley & Sons, New York, 1957), pp. 54 ff., calls for a typology of national actors.

its power permits, take some action to redress its grievances and thus fall into the "revisionist" category, irrespective of the personal characteristics of its leaders or the peculiarities of its national culture. Victors who fail to foresee this reaction on the part of the vanquished are in for a rude awakening.

Yet it would be a mistake to ignore the impact of individual or national differences on the behavior of states that express dissatisfaction with the *status quo*. One must expect deviations from any general pattern discovered by means of deduction. The case of German "revisionism" after World War I offers a good illustration. Before Hitler came into power, Germany, under democratic leaders, was already demanding redress of certain grievances. Yet had the democratic leaders remained in power, they might well have refused to satisfy their demands by means of war, even if Germany had become as powerful as it did under Hitler — or as powerful as Hitler, in his megalomania, believed her to be. Theory, therefore, must descend below the high level of abstraction at which only "states" are the actors, in order to give consideration to such significant factors as the inclination of dictators to overestimate their nation's power, the ability of demagogues to arouse and make use of popular dissatisfactions, or the reluctance of democratic leaders to initiate war.

II

Up to this point, the discussion has been devoted to criticizing the states-as-actors theory for its neglect of the individuals as actors. Another kind of objection to the theory has been raised on the ground that it fails to allow for the possibility of corporate actors other than the nation-states. It is asked whether a realistic image of the contemporary international scene should not include such non-state corporate actors as the United Nations or the Communist International. If it should, the term multi-state system would no longer be fully adequate to describe the environment in which statesmen and other actors operate in the world today.

The "billiard-ball" model of the multi-state system which forms the basis for the states-as-actors theory leaves no room for corporate actors other than the nation-state. By definition, the stage is preempted by a set of states, each in full control of all territory, men, and resources within its boundaries. Every state represents a closed, impermeable, and sovereign unit, completely separated from all other states. Since this is obviously not an accurate portrait of the real world of international politics, one can say that reality "deviates" in various ways from the model, because corporate bodies other than nation-states play a role on the international stage as co-actors with the nation-states. To the extent that these corporate bodies exert influence on the course of international politics, knowledge about them and about the deviations that permit them to operate becomes indispensable to the development of a well-rounded theory.

More even than in the case of the individual actors, one is justified in using the term "deviation" here to indicate that any important impact of non-state corporate actors constitutes the exception rather than the rule. As things stand today — and are likely to remain for an indefinite period — there can be no serious doubt about the paramount position of the nation-state or about the superiority of its influence and power. Even enthusiastic supporters of the UN can hardly fail to realize that there can be no UN action of any consequence if a single great power refuses to permit it. To date, no non-state corporate actor has been able to rob a nation-state of the primary loyalty of more than a small fraction of its people. If this should ever occur — if, for example, a Communist International could persuade a state's soldiers and workers to refuse obedience to their own national government — the state in question would prove an empty shell when put to the test of war. Occurrences of this kind were well-known in medieval times, before the age of nation-state predominance, when excommunication by the Pope, a supranational actor, could deprive a king of control over his people.

There is no lack of a suitable vocabulary to identify a set of non-state corporate actors, but it is not without significance that all the terms refer to something called "national" which is the characteristic feature of the nation-state. One distinguishes between international, supranational, transnational, and subnational corporate bodies as potential co-actors on the international stage. Some have criticized this terminology on the very ground that it creates a prejudice in favor of the nation-state as the center of things and have suggested that the term "international" politics be replaced by the term "world" politics. However, one is hard put to define where "world" politics begin and domestic politics end, unless the former is designed to comprise acts that transcend national boundaries — which brings one back to the nation-state with its territorial borders.

It is not hard to see what kinds of deviations from the billiard-ball model of a multi-state system are possible, or to see that certain types of deviations facilitate the operations and increase the influence of non-state corporate actors.

If the states of today are not monolithic blocs — and none but the totalitarian states are — groups, parties, factions, and all sorts of other politically organized groups within such states can take a hand in matters transcending national boundaries. They may do so directly, in negotiating and dealing with similar groups abroad or even with the governments of other states, or they may exert their influence as domestic pressure groups so effectively that foreign statesmen would be ill-advised to ignore them. Some democratic states have exhibited such pluralistic tendencies that they offer to the world a picture of near-anarchy. They seem to speak to the world with many and conflicting voices and to act as if one hand — one agency or faction — does not know what the other hand is doing. One can also point to states, some of them new states in the process of consolidation, where integration is so poor that other states must deal with parts, rather than with a fictitious whole, if diplomacy is to be effective.

Another deviation bears on the degree of separateness or, if one prefers, of cohesion between nations. Here, too, one can visualize a wide gamut of gradations. Since World War II, for example, West Germany and France have at times been close to the pole of complete and even hostile separateness; but at other times they have been drawn so closely together that a merger of the two into a single European Union appeared as a practical possibility. While such a union might have become a new super-state, it might instead have remained a more loosely-knit international organization, like the British Commonwealth which can exert considerable influence on the behavior of its members.

Then, again, there are deviations from the complete impermeability of the nation-states envisaged in the billiard-ball model.[5] Some peoples today are shut off from contact with the rest of the world by an Iron Curtain, but the boundaries of most states are permeable, leaving the inhabitants relatively free to organize into groups transcending national boundaries. If they desire, they can do so even for the purpose of exerting international influence. One need only think of the international Communist movement, of international Socialist groups, or of international cartels which have, at times, been able to perform as transnational actors.

Finally, sovereignty, in the political sense of the term, is not everywhere and always as undivided and total as the legal concept would indicate. The behavior of the satellite states within the Soviet orbit, legally recognized as sovereign, can be understood only if the role of the Soviet Union is taken into account, either as a co-actor in the background or as the master actor. Another case of divided sovereignty is presented by the European Coal and Steel Community which can act with considerable independence within the field of its competence.

Whether the United Nations has become a center of decision and action in its own right is a *quaestio facti,* as it is in the case of all the competitors of the state. Theoretically, there is no reason why the real world should not "deviate" from the condition of complete nation-state sovereignty to the point of permitting an international organization, such as the UN, to become a relevant actor. It would have to be recognized as such if resolutions, recommendations, or orders emanating from its organs should, for all practical purposes, compel some or all member governments to act differently than they would otherwise do.

A theoretical discussion of the actors is not the place to answer the question whether non-state corporate actors are presently gaining or losing ground in their competition with the nation-state. But because there has been much speculation about an alleged trend away from the state system and toward an ever-increasing role of interna-

---

5. In *International Politics in the Atomic Age* (Columbia University Press, New York, 1959), John H. Herz uses the term "impermeability" to indicate the protection that the classical nation-state was able to provide until, with the advent of the air and missile age, "the roof blew off the territorial state" (p. 104).

tional bodies, if not of a single supranational world government, it is worth noting that two sharply conflicting tendencies can be detected in the world today: one toward the enhancement, the other toward the diminution of the paramount position of the nation-state. Which of the two tendencies will gain the upper hand in the end depends on so many factors that a reliable prediction seems impossible.[6]

In recent times, the nation-state has been gaining much ground geographically. There is hardly a region left in the world where nation-states are not either already functioning or in process of being established. There has also been a marked increase in the power over men that can be exercised in the name of the state. Never before has the state achieved so complete a monopoly of control within large areas as is enjoyed today by the totalitarian Soviet Union with its Iron Curtain and its ability to radiate ideologically far beyond its own borders. Satellitism and international Communism represent more of a triumph of the Russian state than of a break with the traditional multi-state system.[7]

However, there are other developments, too, which point in the opposite direction. It is not enough, obviously, to point to the impressive array of international and other non-national organizations that have mushroomed in recent years; these organizations may constitute or develop into mere instruments of national policy. Nor is it enough to prove on rational grounds that the nation-state is becoming increasingly less fit to satisfy the needs for security and economic development. However, there is ample evidence to show that the United Nations and its agencies, the Coal and Steel Community, the Afro-Asian bloc, the Arab League, the Vatican, the Arabian-American Oil Company, and a host of other non-state entities are able on occasion to affect the course of international events. When this happens, they become actors in the international arena and competitors of the nation-state. Their ability to operate as international or transnational actors may be traced to the fact that men identify themselves and

6. John H. Herz, *ibid.*, sees two "blocs" replacing the now obsolete nation-state.
7. George Liska, in *International Equilibrium* (Harvard University Press, Cambridge, Mass., 1957) points out that "the trend to horizontally expanding functionalism has been at least equalled by the drive to enlarge the vertical power structures of major states by the addition of dependable allies and dependent satellites" (p. 132).

their interests with corporate bodies other than the nation-state.

Here, there appears a connection between the phenomenon of non-state corporate actors and the individuals-as-actors approach. No deviations from the states-as-actors or billiard-ball model are conceivable unless it is unrealistic to assume that men identify themselves completely and exclusively with their respective nation-states, an assumption that excludes the possibility of non-state corporate actors exerting any influence of international significance. But in order to discover how men in the contemporary world do in fact identify themselves — or what they refer to, as Paul Nitze puts it,[8] when they speak of the "we" in international affairs — attention must be focused on the individual human beings for whom identification is a psychological event.[9] If their loyalties are divided between the nation and other political organizations, such subnational bodies as a domestic political party, such international bodies as the UN, and such transnational bodies as a Communist International can, in principle, become significant factors in the shaping of world events. Tito's actions are often unintelligible if it is forgotten that he identifies himself not only with Yugoslavia but with some loose grouping he calls the Socialist camp. What Arab leaders mean when they speak from the point of view of their primary corporate interest may be a purely national interest or instead a changing composite of national, Pan-Arab, and Pan-Islamic interest. Whether the Pope merits recognition as an actor in world affairs cannot be determined merely by reference to the fact that he lacks the military power states are able to muster. If nations and statesmen do, in fact, act differently when under the impact of orders or admonitions from the Vatican, to disregard the Pope as an actor would mean overlooking a significant aspect of international politics. Similarly, the actor capacity of the United Nations depends on whether the policies of national statesmen are affected by resolutions of the General Assembly, by reprovals of the UN Secretary General, or by orders of the Security Council.

One may conclude, then, that only an empirical analysis, penetrating to the minds of men and to their manner of choosing one

---

8. See Paul H. Nitze's essay, *supra*, pp. 1-14.
9. In Kaplan's words, "Individuals, after all, have no biological ties to the nation" (*ibid.*, p. 157).

course of action over another, can throw light on the role of non-state corporate actors and thus supplement a possibly oversimplified and unrealistic concentration on the nation-states as sole corporate actors. While it would be dangerous for theorists to divert their primary attention from the nation-state and multi-state systems which continue to occupy most of the stage of contemporary world politics, theory remains inadequate if it is unable to include such phenomena as overlapping authorities, split loyalties, and divided sovereignty, which were pre-eminent characteristics of medieval actors. These phenomena, which indicate serious deviations from the billiard-ball model, also deserve attention from the analyst today. Here, too, then, the states-as-actors and the individuals-as-actors theories must supplement each other. If they can be made to do so, they will contribute to the development of a theory that can rightly claim to be "realistic" since it will throw light on all the chief aspects of the realities of contemporary international politics.

Chapter VII

Power and Ideology in National and International Affairs

BY REINHOLD NIEBUHR

EVERY STUDENT of politics knows that political communities and relations must deal with "power" rather than pure persuasion on the one hand or merely with "force" on the other hand. Force may be defined as the physical power to coerce the will against the inclination. It is always an alloy in the structure of power, whether in internal or in external affairs; but power is something much more complex than force.

Power is, in fact, composed of the authority and prestige which gains the implicit or explicit consent of the subject or the ally with a minimal use of coercive force. Pure force may be necessary in conflict situations in which it is impossible to influence the foe; and force, therefore, becomes the *ultima ratio* of conflict. In domestic situations, where the sovereignty of a government rests upon the ability to wield police power alone, sovereignty and tyranny become identical.

Ferrero, in his *Principles of Power,* has taught us to distinguish between legitimate and illegitimate government in terms of the authority of the one to gain either implicit or explicit consent, and the inability of the other to establish authority except by "force and fraud." The significance of this distinction is that it places both democratic and traditional governments in the category of "legitimate" governments. The former relies upon explicit consent for the authority of a particular government, but must also rely on implicit consent for the authority of the system of government which permits the alternation of particular governments by popular will. The latter is more legitimate than pure democrats are inclined to believe because it has enough implicit consent to dispense with fraud and to rely on only a minimum of force. In short, the source of power is the authority of a government to gain consent without force. In international relations, this authority is transmuted into prestige, which is able to win allies and gain cooperation without coercion.

If power is identical with authority, it follows that the climate of a culture or its "ideology," which sanctions a particular type of authority, is really the ultimate source of power. The implicit consent for the system of government which allows alternations of government by explicit consent was established in Western society only through four centuries of tortuous history in which it was proved that such freedom and flexibility was not incompatible with, but actually a resource for, stability and justice. The Western world was rather tardy in proving that justice and freedom were compatible. The fact that the case was not proved in the period of early industrialization in nineteenth-century Europe was responsible for the rise of the competitive ideology of communism.

Before the rise of democracy, legitimate governments drew their authority from various ideological systems which were identical in their emphasis upon justifying the authority of government chiefly by its ability to maintain order, if the order was not bought at too great a price of justice. That is to say that it was taken for granted that the concentration of power in government was a necessary evil, which would result in some injustice. But if the injustice became intolerable, as it did in the later stages of absolute monarchy, the authority of government broke down. In other words, justice is always a secondary, though not a primary, source of authority and prestige. The primary source is the capacity to maintain order because order is tantamount to existence in a community, and chaos means nonexistence.

The ability to maintain order in traditional governments since the rise of the first empires in Egypt and Babylon rested on the authority derived on the one hand from the prestige of continued rule and on the other hand on the prestige gained from the claim that the political order was an extension and an application of the cosmic order. In the one case the "legitimacy" of dynastic inheritance guaranteed the transmission of authority from generation to generation. In the other case idolatrous claims were made for the priest-kings and god-kings of Egypt and Babylon in order that both legitimacy in the narrow sense and in the sense of the ultimacy of the order would guarantee the "majesty" necessary to prevent chaos. In both cases, reverence for an order which a generation could not create but from which it could benefit was involved. This is the religious element in the majesty of government. The priests did not create this reverence for Providence but they could manipulate it. They were, therefore, the chief agents of the "organization of consent" in the ancient empires.

While the rise of Christianity eliminated the explicitly idolatrous element in the majesty of government, it is interesting that political authority in the West, since Emperor Constantine, made religious claims for the source of its authority, and that with the Hildebrandine Papacy the Pope sought to overtop these claims by asserting the supremacy of the sacerdotal. The Protestant Reformation was, at first, so intent on challenging the claims of the pope in the name of the king, and it was so afraid of chaos if the latter's claims were not religiously supported, that the post-Reformation era gave little support for the rise of a democratic ideology. In short, the ideological support for political power, whether of Pharaoh, Emperor, Pope or King, whether in pagan or in Christian cultures, was contained in the twin emphases upon providence: the stability of a dynastic house, transmitting authority through the generations, and its relation to cosmic or divine order and intention. Through all these millenia it was order, and not justice or freedom, which was the primary concern of the architects of the political community. Nevertheless, the modern free society slowly came into being in which the prestige of justice was added to the source of authority, and freedom was made a prerequisite of justice. How did this ideological shift occur? One answer is that the monopoly of power in absolute monarchy or in the papacy became so vexatious that the injustice which was the by-product of monarchial order destroyed the implicit consent by which dynasts ruled. The breakdown of dynastic rule made room for the ideology of an open society in which the "consent of the governed" was made into the ultimate source of authority. Stated in absolutely consistent terms this principle made for either anarchy or tyranny, as it did in the French Revolution: for it is not in the power of each generation to engineer the consent for a system of government but only for a particular government.

A free society must have a proper reverence for the principle of government as a source of order and a proper insistence that the power of government must be brought under control of the people, and that the majesty of government must be partly derived from its capacity for justice. This proper balance was first achieved in the political theories of the later Calvinists and since has been elaborated by both sectarian and secular political theorists, so that modern political authority is derived from the capacity of the ruler to maintain both order and justice. It must be observed that these ideological changes in the approach to the political order were not purely rational or religious. A certain shift in the power relations of the classes was the instrument of the shift. The middle or commercial classes, kept politically impotent in the communities in which priests and soldiers shared dominion from the rise of Egypt to the decline of the Middle Ages, became the real protagonists of the theory of the consent of the "governed" by claiming political power and authority. Commensurate with their growing economic power, they formed a society in which a monopoly of power was not easy for any portion of society, and which gradually proved by tortuous history that this freedom and flexibility could be made the servant, rather than the nemesis, of order. For these commercial classes had created a commercial civilization. In the flexibilities of that new civilization a more flexible instrument of political authority was necessary. Thus through four centuries of Western Christian history, political authority was gradually elaborated which could grant freedom and which needed the prestige of justice as the source of its authority as well as the prestige of being the instrument of order. The culture and climate, the "ideology" which supports democratic authority in the Western world is thus drawn partly from the peculiar flexibilities and necessities of a technical society, partly from the Christian tradition, which valued the individual as transcending any social process and political community, and partly from modern secularism and empiricism which generated the temper of criticism and punctured the religious pretensions which were the source of so much political authority in the past.

The ideological resources of a democratic political authority are, in fact, so various that one is tempted to be skeptical about the capacity of any culture to create this kind of power or authority if it does not possess both the flexibilities and mobilities of a technical society and the ultimate religious presuppositions of the Judaeo-Christian culture. These presuppositions are important because, in contrast to the mystic religions of the Orient, they emphasize the dignity of the individual and his responsibility transcending all political processes and cohesions. The democratic "way of life" faces an original embarrassment in seeking prestige beyond the confines of the West by the fact that it seems a luxury which only our kind of civilization can achieve. The embarrassment increases as we find ourselves in competition and conflict with the communist power precisely on the two continents of Asia and Africa on which the achievements of democracy in making freedom compatible with both justice and stability seem unattainable, at least in the short run, and in which our prestige derived from justice is defective when applied to foreign, rather than domestic, relations.

It would be simple to solve the problem by defining the communist competitor as a power system based upon "force and fraud." It does generate terrible injustices by its monopoly of power and its claims of justice are on the whole fraudulent. But such a solution of the problem is too simple because the communist competitor derives both its political authority at home and its prestige abroad from an ideological system, which, however mistaken, has sufficient plausibility to impress the Colored Continents. Let us, therefore, consider the ideological presuppositions from which the authority of communist governments derive.

The ideological system which makes communism something more dangerous than a system of power based upon "force and fraud" is drawn partly from the sectarian apocalyptic visions of a kingdom of perfect justice and partly from the materialistic but ethically idealistic concepts of "totalitarian democracy" which had their rise in the French revolution. It gained lodgment in the West precisely because a democratic society had not, in the early period of industrialization, perfected its equilibria of power sufficiently to guarantee justice. The authority of democratic governments was challenged on the ground that government was an engine of injustice rather than an instrument of justice. The primary dogma of communism was that government played this sad role because it was an instrument of an outmoded property system which could be abolished only by a revolution. Communism had a secondary dogma according to which the dominant classes of a capitalistic society exploited not only the internal proletariat but the "colonial" nations, that is, the nations of the non-technical world. It is the secondary dogma which concerns us particularly in our ideological conflict with communism on the Colored Continents. We must recognize that this is primarily an ideological conflict. It cannot be solved by appeals to arms even though arms must be held in readiness for the possibility of various conflicts of pure military force.

The ideological situation in Europe is most briefly described by recognizing that the original injustices of a free society have been sufficiently corrected to give the free governments of the Western world sufficient prestige of both justice and stability to make the whole technical civilization practically immune to communism. Significantly, the communist creed is a live option only in the moribund capitalism of France and the semi-feudal culture of Italy. It has, until recently, triumphed in Eastern Europe, partly by sheer force of arms and geographic propinquity, and partly by ethnic "Slavic" sense of kinship, and partly because the economy of Eastern Europe was sufficiently feudal and agrarian to give the communist dogma a certain plausibility. One of the ironic facts of history is that communist dogma hopes for a climax of revolution out of the mounting injustices of capitalism, but actually achieves the greatest plausibility in decaying feudal societies, which have exactly the imbalances of power and resulting injustices which first gave rise to the middle class revolt against the feudal order. In the context of European civilization the very historical complexities which validated the democratic authority served to refute the ideological illusions upon which the communist authority rested.

Developments in the communist empire since the death of Stalin reveal that we are not dealing merely with a system of power but with an ideological system in which the peculiar authority of the communist priest-kings found support and then declined. It could, of course, be defined as a system of "force and fraud," for Stalinism certainly made many fraudulent claims. But it would be more accurate to define it as a power system in which force and ideological illusion supported each other. The illusion was derived from the Marxist apocalypse, according to which governments are merely the agents of property holders, and will wither away when property is abolished. This illusion was very real in the early days of Marxism. The facts of history tended to refute the illusions; and Stalinism may be defined as the system of force and fraud designed to prevent the refutation from becoming known. The intolerable monopoly of power became so vexatious, even to the oligarchies which shared the rule of the tyrant, that they ventured the bold step of discrediting the dead tyrant and admitting the grave injustice which flowed from the monopoly of power. It is clear that though Stalinism was primarily a system of terror, it was still supported by many ideological illusions. That is proved by the decay of authority with the destruction of the Stalin myth. Naturally the decay of authority was most telling in the satellite nations, where a great deal of force, compounded with Marxist ideological illusions, was used to keep the central authority unchallenged. The refutation of the universalistic illusions of the original myth by Russian national interests served to hasten the process of disillusionment. In Poland, the fear of Germany and other factors made it possible to reconstruct the authority on a nationalist-communist or Titoist basis. But in Hungary, where ethnic kinship did not support the Russian authority and where the fear of Germany did not serve to keep the nation loyal to a hated tyranny, the revolution quickly broke beyond the limits of Titoist nationalism and has been cruelly repressed by military force. The catastrophic effect of this development on the communist parties of the West proves that the ideological illusion in the communist dogma was still a considerable source of prestige, even after all the disillusionments of the past decades. The events in Hungary have reduced the political prestige of communism in the West and completely destroyed any remnant of prestige in Hungary so that authority rests purely upon bayonets and machine guns, the ultimate in tyranny.

But it would be foolish to suppose that the refutation of the primary dogma of communism in the context of a technical society had guaranteed a democratic alliance a simple victory in the ideological struggle on the two Colored Continents, where the secondary dogma of communism has never lost a certain measure of plausibility and where colonial and ex-colonial peoples either dreamed of liberty and equality or celebrated their emancipation by residual resentments against a previous domination. For it is a fact that the nineteenth century impingement of the technical West upon the non-technical world was "imperialistic" in the way that power always impinges upon weakness. The prestige derived from domestic justice was not sufficient to obscure the loss of prestige due to imperial dominion, even though that dominion was never as purely exploitative as the communist dogma assumed. The creative elements in the imperialism of the West were, moreover, obscured by the racial arrogance of the white man in his relations to the Colored Continents.

The brutal suppression of Hungarian liberty by the communist power, which finally discredited communism in Europe, was synchronous with the Anglo-French attack upon Egypt which symbolized the evils of "colonialism" to the Colored Continents even though the operation of the Suez Canal by an international authority was hardly as flagrant an expression of exploitation as the Egyptians and Russians pretended to believe. But the British and French attack upon Egypt gave a new ideological plausibility to the communist dogma.

We thus have an ironic historical coincidence. The final refutation of the communist ideology in Europe was synchronous with a very telling seeming proof of the ideology on the Colored Continents. These events in Europe and in Egypt prove that the West cannot be too complacent about the refutation of the communist ideology in Europe when it is still such a vital force on the Colored Continents by the power of its secondary dogma about imperialism.

While the West rather too complacently sought to alleviate, by technical assistance to backward nations, the poverty in which communism ostensibly breeds, the communist entered into competition with us in offering technical assistance, thus revealing that they no longer relied on revolutionary discontent of the "masses" but upon the residual or real resentments of colonial or ex-colonial governments. Thus communism had found allies among hitherto subject peoples and these peoples found a protagonist in the communist power which had learned to master the crafts of a technical society without going through the tortuous self-denying experiences which made a technical civilization in the West the generator of a democratic political order.

The old organic forms of collectivism could exchange their organic forms for the more dangerous forms of technical collectivism, and the technically proficient Russian tyranny could threaten the democratic and technical Western world with isolation on the Colored Continents.

It could even prove more flexible in interpreting its own dogmas than the West, which offered technical assistance to prevent revolutions in Asia and Africa, while the communist offered it to enable dictatorial governments to embrace Western technology without embracing the democratic creed of the West. As a source of internal authority, the creed of democracy was too complex and too varied in its sources to be obviously available to the recently emancipated feudal or pastoral cultures of Asia and Africa. The delicate balances of power which made freedom compatible with justice seemed out of reach to the newly-born nations. At the same time, the ideological support of Western democracy was defective as a source of prestige in external affairs because it was tainted by the memories of the previous impingement of technical power upon non-technical nations, which according to the communist creed could be made to appear as the inevitable consequence of "capitalism."

Domestically, democracy was too difficult and in foreign affairs its ideology was too tainted to have the obvious advantages which the West fondly assumed its creed to possess. In the ideological conflict for prestige between the Western nations and Russia the disadvantages from which the West suffers are more desperate than we have ever admitted to ourselves. In fact, there is a danger that we will be driven into a new fit of hysteria once we recognize the true state of affairs. Since the struggle is not purely ideological we can feel secure for some time under the umbrella of an atomic stalemate. Both sides have admitted that neither side would explicitly risk a global nuclear war.

But these military factors also aggravate our problem. They have tempted us, since the aggression in Korea, to think too much in terms of containing the communist power by military defense pacts. These pacts have cost us the friendship of India and Afghanistan.

While military power is the *ultima ratio* of conflict with a foe, it is clearly not a source of prestige, either for the internal authority of a government or for its relations with other nations. The communist empire has discovered to its cost that the exertion of military power in relation to "allies" is subject to a law of diminishing returns.

In fact the constitution of modern society in a technical age has invalidated most of the sources of authority which governed the authority and prestige of traditional societies. Force has remained as an alloy but not as a basic metal of authority; and its limits as a source of authority are almost as clearly defined in an age which has experienced tyranny as in the age of the dynasts. The prestige of uninterrupted rule has disappeared as a source of authority and the pretension that the political order is intimately related to the cosmic order (the core of the religious element in authority) has evaporated in an age which is acutely aware of historical contingency. There remains only the achievement or the hope of justice as the source of authority and prestige. The hope of justice, or the pretension of having achieved it, is almost as potent as the actual achievement. That is why the communist totalitarianism, with its ideological remnants of utopian hopes, is so rigorous a competitor with democracy for the favor of peoples, particularly on the Colored Continents.

While prudence dictates that we begin our estimate of the ideological struggle between democracy and tyranny on the Colored Continents with an objective consideration of the disadvantages under which the West labors in this competition, we must not adopt a defeatist view from a consideration of these advantages. We must be realistic enough to know that the initial advantages are on the other side, despite the recent self-discrediting of the communist empire. But the ideological struggle may nevertheless be won if we are patient enough to allow historical experience to refute the illusions of the communist dogma and to correct the errors in the approach of technically competent civilizations to technically backward ones.

We must also be resolute enough to protect the free world when it is threatened as it has been in the Middle East by a combination of military power and political chicane. If we do not understand the power-political realities sufficiently to know that whoever controls the Middle East also controls Europe, all ideological considerations will become irrelevant through forces which act more quickly than the slow movements of shifting prestige and the ideological systems which support that prestige.

On the level of ideological conflict we must free ourselves of the burden of the charge of "colonialism" on the Colored Continents.

This cannot be done simply by calling attention to our own anti-colonial past and by inference fastening the charge more securely on our Western allies. Secretary Dulles attempted this gambit in the Suez crisis, with catastrophic results, for it helped Russia and Nasser to defeat our allies in the Middle East, a defeat which they aggravated by military action which failed to unhorse Nasser, precisely because Russia and Nasser could count on us to support them for "moral" reasons. Europe is consequently threatened from the Middle East and we are in danger both of being isolated and of adopting a new policy of pacifist isolationism. We are inextricably bound up with the fate of Europe and we cannot avert this fate by calling attention to the ideological differences between us on the matter of colonialism. We would have a much better chance of winning both the ideological and the power struggle if we discriminated more carefully between those European powers which have creatively extricated themselves from previous colonialism and have tutored hitherto subject nations in good faith for eventual independence and those nations which are hopelessly bogged down in colonialism. Broadly speaking that means the distinction between Britain and France.

Every indiscriminate designation of the European powers as "colonial" by us is bound to support the communist ideological claims and to obscure the great achievement of Britain in liquidating an empire and creating a commonwealth of nations in which Asian nations have equal rights with European ones, and in which even the backward cultures of Africa are being trained in the arts of democracy. This achievement is somewhat clouded by the desperate policies of Britain in the Mediterranean, particularly on Cyprus and the Suez, policies which were, however, dictated by the consciousness of the strategic value of the Mediterranean lifeline and its importance for the whole European economy. We contributed to the desperation by pressing the British to leave Egypt in order to avoid the charge of colonialism. The consequent success of Russia in winning essential control of the Middle East proves that the power struggle must not be too rigorously subordinated to the ideological struggle.

The case of French colonialism is quite different. France was unable to maintain her empire in Indo-China because she could not offer sufficient independence to Indo-China to give moral dignity to the fight against the communists, posing as nationalists. She is now bogged down in a similar stalemate in Africa, trying vainly by force of arms to prove that an Islamic African dependency is really a part of metropolitan France. There is no hope of winning the ideological struggle with the handicap of French failures upon our cause. Since the end of the Fourth Republic and the quasi-dictatorship of De Gaulle it is rather unclear what the French policy is, or will be. De Gaulle evidently wants to change the French Union into a kind of Commonwealth, but it is not clear that Algeria will have sufficient freedom from metropolitan France to be a part of this Commonwealth.

A wise course for us would be not to wage ideological warfare against our two strong European allies in the name of our "anti-colonialism," but to establish a more intimate alliance with Britain so that the two nations which are freer of the ideological handicap than any other may form the core of the alliance of free nations and may gain sufficient prestige to dissuade France from her present course which has such catastrophic consequences in the ideological struggle. Meanwhile, we can confidently expect that the stresses to which the communist empire is exposed in Europe will generate policies of desperation, as in Hungary, and that lingering illusions will more and more be replaced by recognition of obvious fraud. Furthermore, the forum of the United Nations fortunately insures that the force and fraud which communism practices in Europe, because of its low moral and political prestige, will become better known in Asia and destroy its prestige on the Colored Continents where it has long posed as the emancipator from colonialism. Our cause is by no means hopeless, though it is more serious than a comfortable nation is inclined to admit. The safety of the free world requires a much shrewder calculation of both the ideological and power factors than we are accustomed to give them.

It must be emphasized in conclusion that we cannot win the ideological struggle on the Continents where technical civilization is in its infancy if we equate democracy with extravagant forms of individualism, which may be regarded as a luxury which only the richest of all nations, our own, can afford. The rest of mankind must try to develop equilibria of power and a tolerable justice within the framework of freedom and to extend freedom on the base of domestic stability and foreign prestige.